# BLACK HEALTH —
## A POLITICAL ISSUE

The Health and Race Project

# BLACK HEALTH – A POLITICAL ISSUE

## The Health and Race Project

**Ntombenhle Protasia Khotie Torkington**

Catholic Association for Racial Justice
*and*
Liverpool Institute of Higher Education

Catholic Association for Racial Justice
St Vincent's Community Centre, Talma Road, Brixton, London SW2 1AS

Liverpool Institute of Higher Education
Woolton Road, Liverpool L16 8ND

First published 1991
© 1991 N. P. K. Torkington

ISBN 0 95158471 5

*British Library Cataloguing in Publication Data*
A catalogue record for this book is available from the British Library

Typeset by K. G. Farren, Scarborough
Printed and bound in Great Britain by Bell and Bain Ltd, Glasgow

# Contents

*For Simon Anthony Sipho*

# Preface

The successful completion of this report is the result of the combined energies of many people to whom I owe a personal debt. I wish to thank them all, and in particular, the black people who have shared their painful experiences and agreed to have them included in this report to provide evidence of the inadequate and inappropriate provision by the Health Service, in the hope that such evidence will help convince those responsible of the need for change. Members of the Granby Community Mental Health Group who continued the struggle, initiated by the Black Women's Group, and established a Drop-In Centre for mentally disturbed black people; members of the Health and Race Steering Committee who gave unstintingly of their valuable time and served as a useful sounding board for some of the ideas pursued in this research; staff of the Neighbourhood Health Project who helped with an earlier fact-finding pilot study on what black people regarded as priority for research, and their involvement in screening for high blood pressure and diabates; Medical Social Workers in the Royal Liverpool Hospital who collected information on the take-up of hospital services by the black elders; the doctors, particularly of Princess Park Health Centre, who were very supportive and provided useful health-related information; the Local Medical Committee and, the then, Family Practitioners Committee for their support and encouragement. I wish to thank the Merseyside Task Force, the Liverpool City Council and the Liverpool Health Authority for their combined efforts in providing funding towards the Health and Race Project.

In addition, some individuals merit special mention: Margaret Thompson, then Secretary to the Community Health Council, for her supportive work without which it is difficult to imagine that the project would have survived; Elsie Cliff, a long-standing friend, a fount of inspiration and a sounding board for many formative ideas; and Gideon Ben-Tovim, who supervised the Project, for his support and encouragement in adopting a value-committed approach to research.

I recently attended a one-day Seminar on research in which I felt extremely encouraged to learn from some participants that they lack the journalistic touch in presenting their written reports. I am afflicted by a similar inadequacy and if this report is presented in an attractive readable format it is no small thanks to my gifted friends and colleagues whom I have exploited, unashamedly, and who have given unselfishly of their valuable time in reading and re-reading many of the pages. Graham White, Gideon Ben-Tovim and Barney Rooney read the entire manuscript and gave valuable criticisms and suggestions. I am particularly indebted to Nigel Mellor who not only read the manuscript but helped in the structuring of parts of this work and was a valuable source of information on some of those aspects which involved the City Council.

I wish to give my warm thanks to Lorraine Campbell who typed many sections of the first draft, and to express my gratitude to Barbara Davies and Janice Shipman, our Departmental Secretaries, who, uncomplainingly, spent many frustrating hours with a temperamental word-processor and emerged with a professionally produced manuscript. For my own image, I just hope they did not mean it when they said they believed the age of forced labour is still with us! Finally, my utmost felt thanks to my colleagues in the Sociology Department at Liverpool Institute of Higher Education for the team-work approach to our teaching responsibilities, which has provided a supportive network to enable me to have space and time and a tremendous incentive to complete writing up the report. To all these many people I give my thanks, and wish to reassure them that they will not be held responsible for the views expressed in this report.

# Introduction

In this book the searchlight is turned on struggles in the field of sickness and health. The book addresses issues of class and racial inequalities in the political, economic and social system within which some people are condemned to an early death. The theoretical assertions made are underpinned by material from the practical experiences of people, which were collected between 1986 and 1988. The focus of the study is on black people and health. Although the project was based in Liverpool, the issues raised have resonance at both the national and international level. The recommendations call for radical changes in policy formulation and implementation which would benefit all, irrespective of race, class, age or gender.

It may not be common for a final report to be written five years after the beginning of a research project. There are, however, exceptional circumstances which justify delay in this particular case. The first substantial work involved in carrying out the action research was largely complete by October 1988 but two areas of need for initiatives in service provision were identified in the process of the initial study, and although I officially left the project in 1988, it was considered appropriate to allow more time to pursue these before finalising this report. One of these initiatives was the Translation and Interpreting Service, which was eventually set up by Liverpool City Council in 1989, and the other was the Drop-In Centre for mentally disturbed black people, established by the Granby Community Mental Health Group in 1990. The processes involved and the role of action research in setting up these services will be discussed in Part Three below.

The material is presented in three sections. Part One analyses the interrelated issues of class and race and argues that whilst black people share the oppression experienced by white people in the same class, 'race', a socially constructed category, creates an added dimension to the difficulties both black and white people experience. The health service as part of the wider social structure reflects this added dimension. Traditional medical ideology with its victim blaming undertones has an important role in contributing to the health experience of working class black and white people.

The methodology adopted in this project is action research. This is a controversial approach which has been criticised by both conventional academics and radical activists. The former question the academic status of such an approach and the latter view it as reformist and therefore an obstacle to radical change. At the end of Part One, these questions are addressed and the politics of action research are discussed.

Part Two is composed of a variety of Consultative Papers produced and disseminated to relevant organisations in the course of the first two years of the project. The first two papers report on the results of action research in screening for high blood pressure and diabetes in both health and community centres. Paper Three discusses the problems faced by the Somali Community. The poor up-take of hospital services by racial minority elderly people is the subject of Paper Four. Paper Five reports on the evaluation of the Health Authority's interpreting service and argues that a comprehensive and centralised service would be more appropriate in meeting the needs of those whose language is not English. Paper Six is on mental illness: the first section of the paper reviews the general literature on black people and mental illness, and the final section looks specifically at the situation in Liverpool.

Part Three deals with the setting up of the Translation and Interpreting Service and the Drop-In Centre for mentally disturbed black people. At one level these can be considered as the 'fruits of action research'. At another level, however, we have argued that because of the relationship pressure groups have to funding, initiatives resulting from their campaigns tend to fall under the ambit of the funding organi- sation. They become, in common parlance, 'what the organisation pro- vides'. However this 'legitimate ownership' can be stretched to the extreme when some members of organisations, desperate to present a progressive public image, lay unwarranted claims on such schemes, including those they have vehemently opposed. We have called this 'Credit Stealing Syndrome' (CSS). CSS is a familiar feature in most organisations and it operates in different ways depending on the type of the organisation.

In general, voluntary sector projects funded by Innercity Partnership are approved for funding for four years. In the case of the Health and Race project the first application was for two years with a view to evaluating the direction of the project after that time and applying for a further two year period. During the first two years the Health Authority, the body through which funding was secured from Innercity Partnership, insisted that the researchers should report regularly to its Race Relations Advisory Committee. The rejection of this demand on the grounds that no other similarly funded voluntary project was required to do the same deepened the conflict and in consequence the Health Authority declined at that stage to recommend the renewal of the Project's grant. One year elapsed before the grant was renewed. In that year a number of meetings were held involving members of the Health Authority, the City Council, the Racial Minorities Health Group, Innercity Partnership and the Health and Race project, to try and resolve the conflict. For that year the Innercity Partnership provided a small grant for a part-time worker to keep the project ticking over, and full funding for two years was granted the following year. The report from this second phase entitled 'Health and Race in the Voluntary Sector' was published in June 1990 and a further report is due soon.

# Part One
# General Overview

# I. The Race/Class Dimension

In global terms there is an imbalance, a disequilibrium among the members of the human family which allows a minority to enjoy the bulk of the world's resources while the majority make do at best in straitened circumstances and at worst in conditions bordering on, or actually in, absolute poverty. Underlying this imbalance is what Sartre calls 'scarcity' contingent to both nature and man:

> 'The fact is that after thousands of years of History three quarters of the world's population are undernourished. Thus, in spite of its contingency, scarcity is a very basic human relation, both to nature and to man.'[1]

In modern times, however, there is an attempt to attack this disequilibrium on humanitarian grounds or on the grounds of justice (or rather the lack of it). There is, in consequence, a call for a greater drive for equality among the people of the earth, and even more pragmatically by more farsighted Western politicians and businessmen, a call for equality on grounds of enlightened self-interest. But even at its loudest this voice finds it hard to compete with vested interests – economic and political, which would like to keep things basically as they are, while granting the need to make some exceptional gestures at times of evident striking need – famine, floods and crop failure – which threaten death to large numbers of people.

In this global picture the first world of the west rules economically, contrasted to the second world of the Soviet block, and the first and second worlds together are set over against a third world which, depending on the ideology held, is categorised as under-developed; developing; oppressed or exploited by imperial powers. The Brandt Report of 1982 drew sharp attention to the widening gap between the third and the first two worlds. The first and second worlds, the report stated, have between them a quarter of the world's population and yet they share four-fifths of its income. The third world including China is composed of three quarters of the world's population. But even in this division which Willy Brandt has characterised as a North/South divide, there is seen to be creeping a fourth world, the underbelly of the first (and perhaps to some lesser extent the second) world. This underbelly is what Brandt calls:

'Pockets of poverty, and the deficiencies in housing and other services, all the less defensible for existing in the midst of what several commentators have called "overdevelopment".'[2]

In that fourth world the starkly evident exploitation and oppression, the under-developed state of the third world is less clearly or markedly discernible, but is nonetheless discernible and increasingly so when we look at the income differentials. The *Christian Statesman* contrasted the income on which some top directors in Britain live, with the income of people on social security. The highest paid of those directors was on a weekly net salary of £91,612 and an unemployed adult male was receiving £27.05 a week from the Department of Health and Social Security.[3] But low incomes are not confined to the unemployed. The Child Poverty Action Group continues to draw attention to the growing number of people who are caught in what it describes as the 'poverty trap'. These are families who are on very low incomes but, because some members in them are working, do not qualify for various forms of supplementary benefits. They are therefore no better off and sometimes may even be worse off than the unemployed who do qualify for such benefits. According to the Child Poverty Action Group the number of families who were in or on the borders of poverty in Britain in the early 1980s was already approaching a quarter of the total population.[4]

Startling but perhaps expected evidence of the deepening gap between the rich and the poor was revealed in a recent article in *The Guardian*. The article states that:

'Over the past 10 years, the richest percent have seen their total income rise by 346 percent as a result of tax cuts, salary and interest rate rises . . . For each individual in the top 1 percent, the windfall over the 10 years averaged £100,000 purely through tax cuts. In the last 12 months, they have received more than £20,000 each from cuts in income tax, inheritance tax and capital gains tax – just under £400 a week.'[5]

The above windfall makes a very sharp contrast when put against 92 pence a week tax cut given to the poorest 2.5 million tax payers in the same period. Mr. Gordon Brown, then the Shadow Chief Treasury Secretary, who gave the above statistics at the start of the Fair Tax '89 Campaign commented that:

'No government this century has given so much to so few so persistently for so long. These findings show that the beneficiaries of last year's Budget have not been low and middle income earners, whose small tax cuts have been wiped out by large mortgage and price rises.'[6]

In Britain the present economic situation has made the presence of large numbers of people living in or on the borders of poverty, as the Child Poverty Action Group pointed out, visible to all but the most blinkered eye. Class divisions, which an earlier theory of embourgoisement, propounded by Goldthorpe and Lockwood[7] had proclaimed of little significance in post-war Britain, are made more apparent, and gravitating to the bottom are people originating (albeit in many cases several generations and many years since) from former colonies and distinguishable by skin colour. In the pecking order in the fight for resources particularly at a time of intensified Sartrean type 'scarcity' such peoples tend to come last. They are the least considered and tend to suffer more from deprivation in all aspects of their lives. On Merseyside evidence of this deprivation has been well documented by members of the Area Profile Group in their publications on housing,[8] employment,[9] health[10] and social services.[11] This particular disadvantaged position in society, it has been argued, is the result of racism.

## 1. Racism

Racism as a concept has been widely used since the early 1970s and there is now a growing awareness about the extent and the degree of the pervasiveness of racism within British society. But it would appear that there is some confusion about what is actually meant by racism. Quite often in both academic and non-academic settings, some individuals prefix their statements by declaring: 'I'm not racist, but . . .'. Such individuals go on to justify their support for decisions to enforce the law in relation to such situations as the use of crash helmets instead of turbans by Sikhs, or the regulation which states that Asian women should not wear their traditional trouser costumes when employed by institutions which demand the use of a uniform when on duty. Any arguments against the injustice of such decisions are summarily dismissed with 'I don't see why they don't adopt our way of life. After all, when in Rome do as the Romans do'. In saying this such individuals acknowledge neither the power relations contained

17

in that proverb nor the historical dimension of those relations, hence the 'commonsense' interpretations in their conclusion. By asking simple basic questions the power element within the proverb is easily exposed: Why Rome? What happened to those who did not do as the Romans did? Did the Britons follow the proverb when they migrated to the colonies in the Empire days? Answers to these questions will clearly show that, in a historical context, what is being put forward now as a commonsense proverb is no more than a prescription for behaviour to be followed by those who have no power in the relationship. As Zubaida has suggested, in race relations a historical dimension is crucial for two reasons:

> 'One is to do with the fact that present group relations have a history and that many aspects of the present relationships can be better understood by relating them to their history. The second reason is that modern race relations situations can be illuminated by comparison and juxtaposition with the wealth of historical examples of group relations of the type designated 'race-relations' in the modern context. A neglect of these examples often leads to a narrow ethnocentrism and simplistic "commonsense" interpretations.'[12]

When individuals who claim not to be racist are asked who they thought was racist, they immediately point to the National Front, the British Movement, the police or white people who attack black people on the streets, or those burning black people's homes and shops. Such a narrow perception of racism misses the point. This is not to say that when black people are attacked on the streets or are victimised by the police or when their houses are burnt down by racists they are not suffering from racism. They are. But that is one aspect, the aspect that is easily recognised and in general deplored by many people who see it as the work of racist bigots. The other aspect, which affects all black people, is that which is to be found in the structures of British society. How does racism operate at this level?

## 2. Structural Racism

This form of racism is more complex and problematic as it cannot be easily identified as racial discrimination. Indeed this point is illustrated in the work of Smith and Whalley. In their report on housing they suggest that what sometimes appears as racial discrimination may be:

'more typically the accidental by-product of an administrative system which has not been adapted to meet the needs of a multiracial society.'[13]

In 'The Racial Politics of Health', it was argued that although a case for the inertia in large institutions can be made it should also be borne in mind that:

'Administrative systems are run by people and the rapidity or sluggishness with which those systems are adapted is indicative of the attitudes held by the administrators controlling them.'[14]

This point is clearly demonstrated when we look at two inherited diseases – Phenylketonuria and sickle cell. Phenylketonuria is the result of an error in the metabolism of phenylalanine, a substance present in all natural proteins. In the absence of the activity of the hepatic enzyme – phenylalanine hydroxylase – this substance accumulates in the blood in abnormal concentrations and the most serious manifestation of this accumulation is mental retardation. By the end of the first 4 months after birth the affected child is already showing signs of brain damage. Like sickle-cell disease, this condition is genetically transmitted and has an active and a carrier or inactive form. The active form affects 1 in 14,000 and the carrier state affects 1 in 60. But unlike sickle cell, Phenylketonuria virtually only affects white children. The disease was discovered in 1934[15] and by the early 1960s national screening for this condition was already in progress. Now all babies are tested within 2–4 weeks of birth.

In the late 1970s the medical profession had realised that there was more danger of mental retardation resulting from congenital hypothyroidism than from the rare cases of Phenylketonuria. In response to this discovery the Government recommended that routine neonatal screening for hypothyroidism should be introduced nationally. January 1st, 1982 was the date put forward by the Medical Research Council for starting the collection of data for hypothyroidism alongside Phenylketonuria screening.

Sickle cell disease, a form of anaemia which only affects black people, was first noted by the medical profession in Chicago in 1910. The active form affects 1 in 500 and the carrier state affects 1 in 10. But to date no safe drug has been devised to cure the condition, though commentators such as Dawson maintain that it:

'ought technically to be relatively easy to devise a chemical capable of curing what is now known to be a chemical problem.'[16]

Finding a cure may not be as easy as Dawson suggests, particularly if little research is being carried out in this field. But at least neo-natal national screening could easily be done, and, as the Birmingham project has shown, with little cost. Griffiths *et al* used the cells of the blood specimen for sickle cell screening, and the plasma of the same specimen for phenylketonuria and hypothyroidism.[17] Why has there been so little done in this area where so many black people are affected? For explanation one could indeed point to the inertia inherent in huge structural organisations which militate against any change away from long established practices. But this is too generalised an explanation to be satisfactory and cannot tell us how change actually does occur at times, such as in the case of Phenylketonuria. The inertia theory needs to be qualified using concrete examples which do show that racism is implicated even at this level of organisational change.

There is another, more common form of structural racism which has consistently discriminated against black people. This is the indirect discrimination which is evident in the employment policies of most British institutions. The exclusion of black people from these institutions comes about through accepted, legitimate practices which are integral parts of the rules and regulations governing the operation of the organisations. Examples of such practices exist in employment, education, housing, social services etc, etc.

For a long time the Liverpool City Council operated an 'internal trawl' system. Vacancies within the Council were advertised internally and only when no suitable internal candidates were available were such posts advertised publicly. In 1983 this Council employed 29,918 workers, 0.9% of whom were black.[18] The estimated number of black people living in the city was between 7% and 10%. Any attempt to redress this imbalance was not likely to succeed as long as the 'internal trawl' was in operation, and certainly a stated commitment to equal opportunity was a meaningless gesture and quite often dangerous since it gave the impression that something was being done, when in fact racist practices continued to discriminate against black people.

Trade unions have also been involved in 'legitimate' racist practices. The nomination rights system allowed unions to nominate their members to certain City Council manual vacancies. The Council had to accept these nominees without putting them through normal employment procedures. Since many black people are not employed and those who are, are alienated by the racism within the unions and many are not union members, this system meant that they were excluded from those council vacancies where such a system operated. 'Ring-fencing', e.g. only those already employed in the education system could apply, was another area where unions had ensured that new vacancies were monopolised by the existing labour force which was mainly white.

There is another form of indirect discrimination which can be aptly described as creeping racism. This operates through the appointment of part-time workers. In education, in particular, it is common practice to offer individuals a few hours of teaching. Such posts are not normally advertised but usually filled through word of mouth from friends and relatives already employed by the organisation. Since in these institutions the workforce is predominantly white, such opportunities are not available to black people. This practice puts part-time workers in an advantageous position when full-time posts subsequently become available. The experience they have gained as part-time workers gives them a powerful position vis-a-vis other candidates in interviews and more often than not they get appointed to posts when these are subsequently publicly advertised.

In Social Services, indirect discrimination is exemplified in the meals on wheels service which in many areas continue to provide 'traditional' English meals. Although this facility is 'available to all', in effect it is not available to black elderly people who find such meals unacceptable for cultural or religious reasons. Similar forms of discrimination are also to be found in housing. These include the points system, Council nomination rights to Housing Associations, etc, etc. A number of reports have been written demonstrating how such practices have left black people with worse accommodation in the cities. Liverpool City Council has been the subject of some of these reports and a lack of positive response from the City has recently earned it a Non-Discrimination Notice from the Commission for Racial Equality.

Some of these long-standing practices are now being addressed in Liverpool. The internal trawl and the ring-fencing have recently been abolished and there are changes taking place in housing. Attempts are being made in Social Services to meet the needs of racial minorities. But such efforts remain isolated and uncoordinated and not part of an overall strategy aimed at the elimination of racial discrimination.

Another subtle and perhaps even more pernicious way in which racism operates is found within the 'legitimate' framework of rules and regulations. Every organisation has its rules and regulations which inform and direct the way an organisation functions. The enforcement and interpretation of these rules and regulations are left in the hands of those in positions of power. Discrimination in this area does not need to resort to breaking the law. All that is needed is to ensure that the rules and regulations are rigidly applied in the case of those against whom one wishes to discriminate. This form of racism is not only difficult to detect but is also difficult to challenge.

If, for example, a black nurse is suspended for being asleep whilst on night duty, how can that nurse bring up a case of racial discrimination on the grounds that the nursing officer who is applying the suspension is too rigid in the application of the rules and regulations? Similarly, if the police or a traffic warden issues an individual with a ticket for parking on the double yellow lines, that individual cannot argue against the penalty on the grounds that other people have been let off the hook for a similar offence. In both cases the complainant would have to prove beyond reasonable doubt that other people have been let off the hook by the same nursing officer or traffic warden. Such detailed evidence is not easily available unless the individual is involved in monitoring the activities of the officers concerned in this area. But even if one can prove that in the past the rules have not been applied rigidly for similar offences there is still a loophole. The officers can simply admit to having been inefficient in the past and now to have made a resolution to carry out the duties more efficiently. The complainant happened to be the first case in the test of this resolution.

In a tribunal case of racism, the officer would get off very lightly. The most he/she would get is a reprimand for failing to pursue the job efficiently in the past. The complainant would be given minimum compensation and the officer would remain in the organisation sensitised and more efficient in implementing sophisticated ways of discriminating. If he/she continues to be an embarrassment to the organisation, he/she may even get promoted out of that position. Most cases do not reach the tribunal stage. The mammoth task of providing evidence to support the claim of discrimination, coupled with the fact that even if one wins the case there is still a possibility of working with the discriminator, is very daunting for most people. Those in positions of authority know this. They therefore continue to discriminate, knowing that the rules and regulations within which they operate provide them with unmatched protection. Rule rigidification is the most widespread and potent way of discriminating. Racism at this level is extremely difficult to identify. It is experienced by most black people, including those who appear to have 'made it' in the system and yet it remains very difficult to challenge because the mechanisms employed are embedded in the 'legitimate' structures of organisations and society.

There is a further point to be made about rules and regulations, including Acts of Parliament. All these are rarely, if ever, formulated in a neutral climate. Their main objectives are to preserve the interests of the dominant groups. Underneath the veneer of rationality, efficiency etc, in the running of organisations and society for which rules/ regulations and laws/Acts are needed, there are still interest groups which determine policies etc. Acts, rules and regulations are in general made, re-made and amended to meet the current needs of those in positions of power. It is difficult to believe, for example, that the laws protecting private property were formulated by those who had no property. Recently we have seen many legislative changes. Take, for example, the various Immigration Acts, the abolition of the Metropolitan County Councils, the changes to housing benefit and the introduction of the Poll Tax, to name but a few. In whose interests have these been brought into existence? It is not for the benefit of those who are powerless in society.

The Immigration Acts, from 1962 onwards, are a classic example of the formulation and reformulation of laws with the effect of benefitting some and disadvantaging many others. To qualify for British citizenship, one of a person's grandparents or parents must have been born in Britain. Given the history of the British Empire it is not likely that many black people would qualify. But the Acts do make provision for white people from former British Colonies to enter and settle in Britain freely.

The Government's unease with the role of County Councils centred on several issues. Most of them were Labour controlled and as a result had introduced a range of policies and programmes which ran counter to the political philosophy of central Government: for example, low cost public transport, sponsorship of the Arts and community-based activities and the promotion of economic development, including co-operatives. The fact that many of these initiatives were taking place on the Government's own doorstep in London meant that the abolition of the Greater London Council was the principal target of the legislation. The introduction of changes in the Housing Benefit arrangements quickly revealed that many elderly people in rented accommodation had savings in excess of the initial £3,000 limit, which thereby debarred them from benefit. The fact that a significant proportion lived in Conservative constituencies on the

South Coast in sufficient numbers to render currently safe seats at best marginal, was clearly influential in encouraging a swift 100% increase in the savings limit.

The reality of how laws, regulations etc. operate is, however, shrouded in an ideological cloud. When in operation they are given a sacrosanct status, a legitimacy which not only distances them from their origin, but also from those who apply them. In essence it becomes immaterial whether or not an officer applying them is racist, sexist, or classist. The system is itself run on a discriminatory framework. This is bad enough, but on occasion it becomes worse. This is when victory is scored by those against whom the law discriminates. Those in positions of power respond by changing the law to block the loopholes or some oversight in the initial provision. An example is the recent case of charge-capping in the Community Charge involving the two London boroughs of Haringey and Lambeth. The former has seemingly lost its battle, leaving the Government content, whereas Lambeth, still embroiled in legal arguments, appears to be winning. The Government has already indicated, however, that it will change the rules if the judiciary eventually rule in favour of Lambeth. This proves that the search for real justice within the legal system must fail, since judgements which do not serve the political interest of the Government of the day inevitably lead to legislative changes which restore conformity with those political interests. There are many many examples where individuals or organisations discover to their detriment the meaning of 'The Golden Rule' – he who has the gold makes the rule.

It is for all these reasons that in challenging any form of discrimination on whatever grounds, the fight should not stop with those who apply and interpret the laws, rules and regulations but must go further and call for the dismantling of all discriminatory laws and regulations. This is not to advocate a society without laws, or organisations without rules and regulations. But these must be formulated in a genuine spirit of democracy, equality and justice and they must be the subject of evaluation in consultation with all those who will be affected by their implementation.

## 3. Racism in the National Health Service

Racism, as demonstrated above, is part and parcel of all British institutions. Our main concern here is with the Health Service. What are the racial politics of health? To answer the question effectively one needs to look at the Health Service as an institution, focussing in particular on the power structure and the ideology underpinning its structure. This will make it possible to see the general relationship between the National Health Service and its users irrespective of the colour of their skin. This broader perspective will provide a background against which to examine the race dimension.

The National Health Service is just one of the many institutions within the umbrella of the Welfare State. The Welfare State itself has so far failed to win a universally held view as to its role in society. For some people it has a positive image. It is seen as a benevolent aspect of a capitalist system which ensures that those who cannot compete in the 'market situation' are not left without the basic necessities of life. Others however, point to its exploitative function. They argue that within the capitalist system, workers are paid a family wage to make sure that the children, who are the future units of labour, are well fed and clothed. In this way, Capitalism is assured of an undying healthy labour market. But, as some people are not employed, the Welfare State provides the basic necessities to enable the reproduction of workers even amongst those whose income falls below the family wage level. To others the Welfare State is a form of social control, a containment which prevents people from revolting against the injustices of a capitalist system. The 'crumbs' of the Welfare State make them feel they still have a stake in the system. If people feel and believe that they have nothing to lose they will be more prone to revolt against their oppression. For those who hold this view the current unprecedented assault on the Welfare State by the Conservative Government is seen as a dangerous path to pursue. As more and more people are stripped of their welfare rights, the experience of the reality of the inequalities and oppression in their lives becomes more stark and in their view this could trigger a process which could lead to the downfall of the Tory regime. This reasoning is flawed and unfair because in effect it suggests that society is somehow justified in not challenging the inequalities which exist in the hope that those who experience them most sharply will rise up in revolt and rid society of an oppressive regime. The likelihood of such an uprising is in any case remote because the process of 'pauperisation' which eventually will affect a large section of the community, including those who are not in receipt of state benefit, is subtle and insidious. But initially the effect is that the least powerful are ideologically isolated from the rest of society. In that way the assault on them is made to appear as the result of their own inadequacy and fecklessness. Their revolt therefore will

25

be thwarted not only by Government forces but also by those who should be allies but who, at the moment, fail to recognise the onslaught that is being directed at their own economic, political and social positions. Rising levels of home ownership and the privatisation of what were publicly owned assets such as telephone, gas, water and electricity, have beguiled many into believing that they are now beginning to share in the country's wealth. But Gordon Brown's statistics quoted earlier clearly illustrate that the present regime is interested only in the numerically small elite section of society. Laws are made and re-made to cater for this group. In the case of the Poll Tax, many families living in small terraced properties with several adults on low pay have been faced with exorbitant charges (well in excess of £2,000) compared to rich individuals living in mansions whose community charge was more likely to be only hundreds of pounds. Income tax cuts, inheritance and capital tax cuts as well as interest rates are, as Gordon Brown stated, further evidence which suggests that the present Government is interested in improving the economic, political and social position of only very few people in society – those who already have more than they need to survive.

Whatever view one takes of the role of the Welfare State there is enough evidence to show that black people get less of the 'crumbs' than do their white counterparts. The literature produced in this area indicates the existence of inadequacies in housing, social services, education and health. In the first three, i.e. housing, social services and education, some form of dialogue has and continues to take place between community groups campaigning for change and those formulating policies or putting those policies into practice. It has been suggested that it is naive to think such discussions have potential to lead to meaningful change. It is true that as a result of pressure, attempts have been made to put 'race' on the agenda of policy-making. But at best, these attempts have produced ad-hoc piecemeal results in terms of provision for black people. In most cases they remain marginal and ineffective. At worst the attempts are dangerous because they give the impression that the institution is 'doing something' and therefore that it is unreasonable to label it racist. In this sense, race-related policies which are not put into meaningful practice serve as a protective cover allowing the institution to sit back and make no real change.

Rooney has argued that real change in relation to race issues is a threatening challenge for most institutions and organisations. The threat, 'arises at a personal level in ideological components and at a personal and organisational level in the potential costs of resolving the challenge of bringing about racial equality.'[19]

In his book *Racism and Resistance to Change*, Rooney analyses the Liverpool City Council Social Services Department (SSD) and looks at the response of this institution to the call for change. In his conclusions, based on a number of case studies, he stresses that the costs involved in implementing policies leading to a meaningful change are plentiful:

"... there is the whole gamut of financial costs of developing new services, staff, training, buildings; the cost of the disruption to the running of the SSD involved in any change, but with a particular edge when being carried out in relation to the Black Community; and the cost of loss of levels of service to the White Community if there is a redistribution of employment and service which in the predictable absence of substantial growth in social services budget would be a necessary indicator of equality. The avoidance of these costs is at the base of the SSD's resistance to substantial change. In responding in some way, because CCETSW (the Central Council for the Education and Training of Social Workers) says so, or because it is believed that change is a good thing, or because of political or community pressure, cost avoidance is crucially shaped by ideological factors.'[20]

The resistance to change syndrome which Rooney describes so succinctly within the SSD holds true of all the institutions. It is precisely the prospect of those costs which is at the heart of a multiplicity of strategies which never get translated into practice. But such resistance should not act as a deterrent. On the contrary, it should be an indication that pressure at every level must be maintained until substantial change is achieved, even if at times the journey to that change is through ad hoc, piecemeal initiatives. Although all institutions resist change, they differ in the extent to which they accept that the problem of racism does exist and must be challenged. In recognising racism as a problem, some mileage has been made in other institutions, but this does not appear to be the case in the area of health care. Here the racial ideology of which Rooney writes, which is expressed 'in a direct way, in antipathy, hostility or assumptions based on stereotyping', remains strong and is re-worked within a power structure which historically has discriminated against the most powerless members of society. That power and the discrimination that emanates from it is to a large extent concealed by the ideological portrayal of the National Health Service as a 'caring' institution. In order to penetrate the veneer of the notion of indiscriminate care for all, let us first look at the power structure within the Health Service. Later, we shall focus on the ideology that shapes practice within the structure of the National Health Service and then we shall see how that practice is experienced by Black people.

## 4. The power of the Medical Profession

If we look at Table 1 and follow the black unbroken lines, the level of power exerted by different groups within the Health Service becomes clear. The Secretary of State has, of course, the overall power. But, compared to other groups the position of the medical profession is very powerful. Doctors have direct representation/access to the Secretary of State. They influence policies at both Regional and District level as well as in the area of Primary Health Care. Within hospitals, consultants remain the most powerful group within the Health Care Team. They own beds. To know more about the detailed politics of 'bed ownership', one needs only to talk to other Health Care Team members such as Social Workers and nurses, as well as general practitioners trying to find hospital beds for their patients. For the end results of that 'bed ownership' syndrome, one needs only to talk to patients who are at the receiving end of the effects of those politics.

Consultants not only 'own beds', they also 'own patients'. The phrase 'my patients' means precisely that. Through what one can only describe as a professional 'gentlemen's agreement', NHS patients do not have the freedom to swap from one consultant to the other. This remains the case even when the patient is dissatisfied with or has no confidence in the consultant with whom she/he is registered. The following story told by the patient who was involved in the situation illustrates how the 'ownership syndrome' at both bed and patient level works.

Mrs. X was a white middle class professional woman who was at the time pregnant with her second baby. As far as she, the midwife who attended her, and her GP knew, the pregnancy had no complications and an unproblematic delivery was predicted. Mrs. X therefore requested a quasi-home delivery, whereby her district midwife would bring her into hospital when in labour, attend to her during delivery and then take her back home as soon as the delivery process

**Table 1   The New NHS Power Structure**

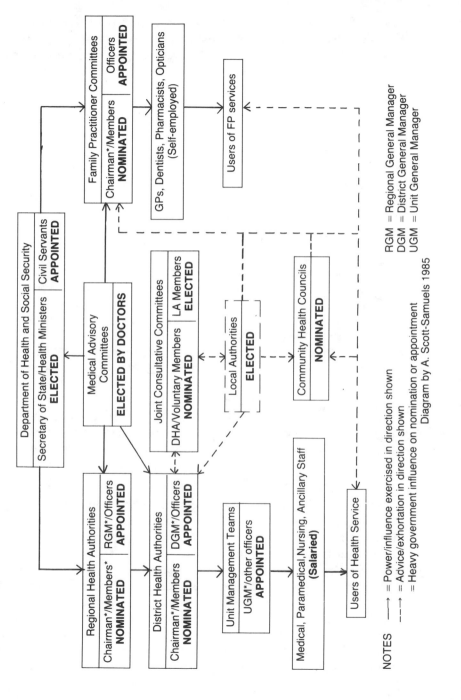

NOTES

$\longrightarrow$ = Power/influence exercised in direction shown

$- - \rightarrow$ = Advice/exhortation in direction shown

= Heavy government influence on nomination or appointment

Diagram by A. Scott-Samuels 1985

RGM = Regional General Manager
DGM = District General Manager
UGM = Unit General Manager

was ended. This, as far as Mrs. X knew, had been agreed with all those involved including the consultant.

When she was over eight months pregnant, she went to the hospital ante-natal clinic to see her consultant for a final visit before delivery. Those who have visited ante-natal clinics will be familiar with the routine, which ends up with the woman lying on her back in a cubicle with nothing on, feeling extremely nervous and vulnerable, in need of reassurance about her own health and more particularly about the welfare of her unborn baby. Mrs. X was not particularly nervous, as she had been assured all along that all was well. But she was lying on her back wearing nothing except a paper gown and a sheet which was removed during the examination. She certainly was not prepared for what happened:

'Mr. F (her consultant) entered the cubicle, with medical students, nurses and a houseman. He said nothing to me, and directed all his comments to the students. He looked at my case notes and then examined me. He then said to the students "We will have to bring her in, she must have a hospital delivery". At this point I raised my head and said "Could you please tell me why I have to be brought in?" Mr. F became very angry and his face turned red and he wanted to know what right had I to question his decision. "Who do you think you are?" and said something about these middle classes who think they can question a doctor's decision. Did I not realise that what he was saying was for the good of my baby? He then turned to the Sister and said: "What is this hospital coming to when patients think they can question doctors' decisions?" By the time he finished his tirade, which was in a loud voice, I was shaking like a leaf and reduced to tears. As he left the cubicle he said "Sister, take her blood pressure again".'

Of course, when Mrs. X's blood pressure was taken it was sky high. The Sister and the houseman then explained to her that when she had first had it taken it had been a bit raised but not significantly, which is the reason they had not mentioned it to her. They too were taken aback by the behaviour of the consultant. But such is the power of consultants that no one challenged what was a blatant assault on the patient by someone whose professional duty is to provide 'care'.

Mrs. X rightly refused to have anything to do with this consultant and demanded to be transferred to another doctor. It was at this stage that the problem of 'ownership syndrome' surfaced. None of the other consultants was willing to have her transferred to them because she was Mr. F's patient. Mr. F was adamant that if she was no longer his patient she could not use one of his beds even if it was empty. Mrs. X informed her G.P. that she would have her baby at home rather than be under Mr. F. Luckily for Mrs. X she had a very good supportive G.P. in her health centre who fought for her until the system gave way and Mrs. X had her baby in hospital under a different consultant. If this happens to a middle class professional white woman, what happens when one is working class and/or black?

At the primary health care level the power relationship vis-a-vis the patient is not very different. Doctors continue to have the upper hand. Their status as independent contractors in the National Health Service and the power that position gives them has been well documented.[21] They have the freedom to accept or reject patients for inclusion in their lists. They have the power to strike patients off their list and they are not obliged to give any reasons for their decision to do so. They can do a great deal to prevent the establishment of services for patient care in their area. A relevant example here is the struggle by the Speke Women's Action Health Group for the establishment of a health centre. For years this had been denied to their area because doctors were against it. The success of that struggle was shown in the Channel 4 documentary 'Healthy cities to live in'. But even in that programme, viewers were not shown the realities of the power relations: some of the Speke doctors put up massive resistance, despite the evidence produced by the women of the appalling conditions under which health care was provided.

It would be a gross misreading if what has been said so far is interpreted as a general condemnation of all doctors. Nothing can be further from the truth. Within the medical profession there are many conscientious, caring and trustworthy people. What is said here is not so much about individuals but about the structure within which they work, and the professionalism which places them above those who consume the services they provide. There is no shortage of individuals who abuse their positions of trust and rightly deserve to be labelled 'nasty'. The point made here, however, is that those 'nasty' individuals are able to abuse their power because they work within a system which allows them to do so. But even more worrying is the patient's knowledge that a caring, conscientious doctor can, and indeed some do, turn 'nasty' and use his/her power when challenged by a patient. The power of the doctor is always a reality in the situation. It is the doctor who decides whether or not to use it. That fact is known by both doctor and patient. It is that knowledge which

31

tips the balance and leaves many patients, who may be dealing with the most caring and conscientious of doctors, vulnerable and power-less in a doctor/patient relationship.

Over and above their professional position, which serves as a source of power, doctors also have societal power which comes from their structural background. Although there is now a fair sprinkling of working class people, women and black people in medicine, the majority of doctors remain middle class white males. The figures from *Health and Personal Social Services Statistics for England* (1990 edition) show that the medical profession is dominated by men. Given the existing classism, sexism and racism in education and employment, it is not unreasonable to assume that these males will also be predom-inantly middle class and white. They control and exert power in strategic and prestigious areas within the profession. Policies affecting health care are formulated at this level and it is reasonable to speculate that these policies will not strongly reflect the kind of health care needed by working class people, women or black people. The very parameters of health care are set within a capitalist middle class framework to the extent that even when working class people, women and black people enter the profession, no matter how radical they may be, their radicalism is soon blunted by their environment. If they overcome the hurdle of ideological constraints acquired through professional socialisation, they will certainly fall when they hit the financial barrier which determines how resources are allocated, or the general professional harassment from colleagues who want to main-tain the status quo within the profession. Although in the late 1980's the power structure of the medical profession was rocked by new government policies, the power relationship between doctors and their clientele has not altered much and the same old medical ideology remains the dominant guiding principle in the relationship.

## 5. Medical Ideology

The western capitalist middle class framework is the basis from which emanates the ideology that is predominant in the medical profession. That ideology is reflected in the medical definition of health. Health is defined in terms of the malfunctioning of a chemical system and treatment is usually seen to consist of chemical, surgical or even electrical intervention to restore the normal functioning of the machine.[22] As Doyal points out, this approach puts emphasis on the ability of individuals to undertake whatever is expected in their social position and it ignores the subjective feelings of depression, anxiety or any other illness which does not grossly interfere with the productive capacity of the individual. We therefore end up with a definition which sees good health as 'the absence of incapacitating and externally verifiable pathology'.[23]

In line with the capitalist middle class ideology which emphasises individualism, the medical model of health not only treats people as mere productive units, but by concentrating on curative rather than preventative medicine, it also reduces the aetiology of disease to the individual level; and even when recognition is given to the role of environmental factors this usually takes the form of victim blaming, a syndrome in which the 'life-style' of individuals or groups is held responsible for the degree of ill health they suffer. Such selective and narrow interpretation of environmental factors is not only misleading but functional in emphasizing 'those aspects which can be seen as the individual's own responsibility'.[24] In a society which puts emphasis on individual responsibility it is not surprising that this approach has gained popularity. As Navarro observed:

> '. . . this life-style politics complements and is easily co-optable by the controllers of the system and it leaves the economic and political structures of our society unchanged. Moreover, the life-style approach to politics serves to channel out of existence any conflict ing tendencies against these structures that may arise in our society.'[25]

In the field of health, the 'life-style' ideology has divided people into categories: the 'worthy' and the 'unworthy'. It is right and fitting to spend society's resources on the former but not on the latter because they have themselves to blame for their ill-health. In the first category are individuals who are intelligent and know how to look after their health. They eat the right food, do the right exercises and have the willpower to resist health damaging habits such as smoking and drinking. They are sexually responsible and knowledgeable about contraceptives. When pregnant they use ante-natal clinics and use child care clinics for their off-spring. They take advice from health professionals and are generally well-informed about their health. If they become ill, therefore, it is not their fault and everything must be done to restore their health.

By contrast, individuals in the second category are thought not to be interested in their health. They are feckless, resistant to medical advice, and are not keen on healthy eating and exercise. They are

B

sexually irresponsible with no interest in contraception and as a result produce many children. They do not use ante- or post-natal clinics and their children are not taken to baby clinics. The unworthy are easy to identify because they have certain characteristics. Kenny, describing a similar categorisation affecting people in housing, gave six such attributes. The 'unworthy' tend to be unemployed, have large families, be in rent arrears, have dirty homes, live in 'high risk areas' and be single parents. In housing, such clients are not given good accommodation because they are seen not to be worthy of society's resources.[26]

The above division is class-based. Middle classes fall in the first category and working classes in the second. The division has a long history in British society but was more explicit in the nineteenth century and was made more prominent in the works of the Eugenicists who specifically wanted to preserve the 'worthy' members of society. In her doctoral thesis Clarke has given a good account of the Eugenics Movement. Only those parts of Clarke's analysis which are pertinent to the medical profession will be discussed here.

Eugenics is about selective breeding. Some of the people involved in the Eugenics Movement had as their main aim the creation of a superior race. This was to be achieved by encouraging prolific reproduction among the 'fit' and discouraging it among the 'unfit'. Clarke states that this desire was concretised in March 1921 when Marie Stopes, a member of the Eugenics Society, opened the first birth control clinic in England in a working class district in London. It is generally believed that Stopes wanted to help working class women who found themselves burdened with endless, sometimes unwanted pregnancies through lack of contraception. This may be true. But, argues Clarke, Stopes does not appear from her own pronouncement to have been too concerned about those women deemed 'unfit'. In 1920 she stated:

'Society allows the diseased, the racially negligent, the thriftless, the careless the feeble-minded, the very lowest and worst members of the community, to produce innumerable tens of thousands of stunted, warped and inferior infants. If they live, a large proportion of these are doomed from their very physical inheritance to be at the best but only partly self-supporting, and thus to drain the resources of those classes above them which have a sense of responsibility. The better classes, freed from the cost of the institutions, hospitals, prisons and so on, principally filled by the inferior stock, would be able to afford to enlarge their own families, and at the same time not only to save human misery but to multiply a hundredfold the contribution in human life to the riches of the State.'[27]

For the 'unfit', amongst whom Stopes included children of mixed race parentage, sterilisation was the answer to ensure the perpetuation of a superior race. Stopes belonged to the Society for Constructive Birth Control and Racial Progress. Her birth control clinic found great sympathy in the eugenics lobby, and among prominent figures supporting her was first the holder of the Charles Booth Chair of Social Sciences at Liverpool University – Professor Alexander Carr-Saunders.[28]

The race and class link was made more explicit in the writings of other Eugenicists who not only desired a superior race for England, but a superior white race to rule the world. Black people were perceived to be innately inferior and were to be driven out of their lands in order to enable the innately superior race to rule. Pearson, a strong force behind this school of thought, believed that in the colonies, including South Africa, the superior white race should dominate the indigenous population even if this meant genocide for the latter.[29]

Other Eugenicists, however, were more concerned about the tainting of white blood by the inferior races in Britain. Reverend James Hamilton, for example, warned against such pollution, which he saw as an undermining element in British power and influences:

'If, for example, the policy be continued of keeping an open door for every foreigner, and especially allowing such alien and inferior breeds as Negroes, Chinese and Japanese to enter, marry, and settle down in great numbers, while young people of pure British blood emigrate to other lands, this country will in a few generations have so much foreign and undesirable blood in the national veins as cannot fail to have a deleterious effect on the national character, and, as a consequence, on all those national ideals, endeavours, and achievements which we value so highly in the present day.'[30]

It may indeed appear far-fetched to link the medical ideology within which individuals are seen as the problem with the ideas contained in the Eugenics Movement. But the discrepancy disappears if we locate professionally and structurally some of those who were active members in the Movement. There was Sir James Barr, President of the British Medical Association; Dr. E. W. Hope, Medical Officer of Health in Liverpool; Humphrey Rolleston, Physician-in-Ordinary to

George V, Dr. C. V. Drysdale, President of the Malthusian League. For Drysdale the link between medicine and Eugenics was the solution to curbing the numbers of the 'unfit'. He suggested that the medical profession should have two oaths – the Hippocratic Oath and a Darwinian one, promising to save the lives of the 'unfit' only if there is no possibility for them to reproduce. To this end he emphasized that:

> 'Success in the environment is the true test of fitness and all those who fail either through disease, accident, or inability to gain a livelihood are the unfit whose lives may be preserved but only at the price of renouncing the right to perpetuate their type.'[31]

Dr. Drysdale's views may be dismissed as unenlightened and outrageous. But do they differ from those held today by some medical professionals who are willing to give some women (working class/ black) an abortion only if they agree to be sterilized? Other Eugenicists who may not have had a direct link with medicine were nevertheless powerful figures within the class structure of British society. The list in Clarke's work includes well-known names such as John Maynard Keynes, Julian Huxley who was once Director-General of UNESCO, Cyril Burt of the now discredited IQ test, Janet Chance and Lady Freda Laski. These personalities were of the same class and hence shared an ideology with other class members who were in powerful positions to influence the medical profession. It is reasonable therefore to argue that the present medical profession has within it ideological strands whose roots are in the racist class structure of British society via the articulated views of the Eugenics Movement.

This then was the climate into which black people came in the 1950's. They were introduced into a society already divided into the 'fit' and the 'unfit'. They were the 'unfit' and like the working classes, were responsible for their own ill-health. But there was a difference. Long before their arrival their status had already been determined by the historical processes of slavery, colonialism and imperialism. That history set them apart and made them more vulnerable and they were perceived to be even less deserving of society's resources than the white working class. That distinction still exists and is felt more acutely by black women who strongly believe that the medical profession is intent on limiting the birth-rate of the black population in order to reduce its numbers.

'There are a lot of doctors who don't even bother to make a secret the fact that they go along with the idea that we are sapping this country's resources, and see it as their professional duty to keep our numbers down. They say things like "Well, you've already got two children, so why do you need to have any more? You might as well get your tubes tied when you come in for that D & C". It's only when you hear Black women talking you realise that it's not just about bad resources or neglect. It's about racism. They don't want us here anymore and they don't need our kids to work for them, so it's easier just to quietly kill us off.'[32]

There are, however, many 'enlightened' doctors who have no tendency towards the form of genocide quoted above. These doctors see the differential experience of health care between black and white people as a function of other factors: if black people suffer more ill-health than white working class people, it is because of their culture or genetic structure. They do not accept that racism, which ensures that black people receive a smaller share of all society's resources and which ultimately determines not only the degree of good health but also the quality of the health care which they receive, is the root of that differential health experience. But this racism cannot simply be reduced to an individual doctor's behaviour or opinion. What is argued here is that at a structural level it is the ethos and the ideologies held by the profession as a whole which defines and shapes the health care made available to different groups. The behaviour of individual doctors must of necessity be analysed in the context of that structure which in turn must be understood as a product of a wider social, political and economic structure.

It is hoped that this section has provided a broader perspective to the understanding of the experience of black people in the health service. It also explains why black people do not accept cultural and genetical explanations for their ill-health. It was against the background of that disbelief that the Health and Race Project was established in Liverpool in 1985.

## References

1. Sartre, Jean-Paul, *Critique of Dialectical Reason*, NLB, 1976, p. 123.
2. Brandt, W., *North–South: A Programme for survival*, Pan Books, 1982, p. 50.
3. Robinson, J. *et al* (ed.), *Christian Statesman*, Manchester, Spring 1984.
4. Child Poverty Action Group, *Poverty, What Poverty?*, CPAG, 1984.
5. *The Guardian*, 1st March 1989.

6. Ibid.
7. Goldthorpe, D. and Lockwood, J. H. *et al*, *The Affluent Worker*, Cambridge University Press, 1968.
8. Law, I. *et al*, *Race and Housing in Liverpool: a research report*, CRE, 1984.
9. Ben-Tovim, G. (ed.), *Equal Opportunities and Employment of Black People and Ethnic Minorities on Merseyside*, Area Profile Group, Liverpool University, 1983.
10. Torkington, N. P. K., *The Racial Politics of Health – A Liverpool Profile*, Area Profile Group, Liverpool University, 1983.
11. Rooney, B., *Racism and Resistance to Change*, Area Profile Group, Liverpool University, 1987.
12. Zubaida, S., *Race and Racism*, Tavistock, 1970, p. 3.
13. Smith, D. J. and Whally, A., *Racial Minorities and Public Housing*, PEP Broadsheet No. 556, September 1975.
14. Torkington, N. P. K., *op cit*, p. 32.
15. Vaughan, V. C. *et al* (ed.), *Nelson Textbook of Paediatrics*, W. B. Saunders Company, 1979.
16. Dawson, G., 'Sickle Cell Anaemia: The Black Killer', *Race Today*, September 1974, p. 274.
17. Griffiths, K. D. *et al*, 'Neonatal Screening for Sickle Haemoglobinopathies in Birmingham', *British Medical Journal*, Vol. 284, 1982, pp. 933–935.
18. Ben-Tovim, G. (ed.), *op cit*.
19. Rooney, B., *op cit*.
20. Ibid.
21. Taylor, C., 'Primary Care in Liverpool', *Radical Community Care Medicine*, Autumn 1981.
22. Doyal, Lesley, *The Political Economy of Health*, Pluto Press, 1981.
23. Ibid, p. 34.
24. Ibid, p. 35.
25. Quoted in Doyle, Lesley, *op cit*, p. 36.
26. Lecture to M A Students in Ethnic Studies in Liverpool University by John Kenny, Director of Housing.
27. Quoted in Clarke, H., unpublished PHD thesis, Liverpool University, 1989.
28. Clarke, H., *op. cit.*
29. Ibid.
30. Quoted in ibid.
31. Ibid.
32. Bryan, B. *et al*, *The Heart of Race: Black Women's Lives in Britain*, Virago, 1985, pp. 104–105.

# II. Politics in Action Research

## 1. The Health and Race Project

Although this research project was set up in 1985 its history goes back to 1982 when the Racial Minorities Health Group was established. The aim of the Group was to investigate the health needs of racial minorities in Liverpool and to evaluate to what extent health services were accessible and acceptable in these communities.[33] After many attempts to secure funds the Group received a grant from the Inner-city Partnership. The project was managed by the Sociology Department in the University of Liverpool and it had an initial life of two years. From the outset this research project was oriented to action since the aim was not only to investigate but to influence or change health policies in order to make them more relevant to all communities in the city. To that extent it ran counter to the predominantly accepted norms and practices of traditional academic research of the social sciences.

## 2. Research in the Social Sciences

In social science research there is a long standing debate concerning notions of objectivity and value freedom traditionally linked to the name of Max Weber.[34] Within academic institutions notions of objectivity and value free research in social science still hold strong sway in terms of academic respectability. As Ben-Tovim *et al* point out, researchers in this perspective are expected to be aloof and uncontaminated by direct 'intervention in political action or policy-making'.[35]

Consequently some of those who venture into the real world of politics or policy formulation find that their academic prowess is questioned by their more traditional colleagues or that they themselves face personal dilemmas of value free or value committed research. Such a dichotomy, suggests Becker, is false because it rests on the assumption that it is indeed possible to have research that is totally free of personal as well as political sympathies. The crucial question for Becker is therefore 'not whether we should take sides, since we inevitably will, but rather which side we are on'.[36] The same point is made by Bulmer who argues that: 'A neutered, valueless, social science is an impossibility.'[37]

Like Becker, Bulmer stresses that central to social science research is the understanding of how far and in what ways such values enter, for lack of this awareness of the value dimension can have a crippling effect on research. In the field of race relations the same point is made more forcefully by Ben-Tovim *et al*:

> 'A more direct political involvement in the process of policy develop-
> ment is necessary if research products are to have any clear
> impact, and indeed the research that does not have a built-in
> political direction and implementation programme will almost
> inevitably be ineffectual. Unfocussed or abstract research of this
> sort, is not, as some may suggest, a-political. All research has
> implicit political objectives and values, we would maintain, and a
> research practice that appears to be examining race relations
> processes but that is not designed to effect any change contains its
> own set of political values, which must ultimately consist of an
> acceptance of the racial status quo.[38]

Black people have, from the outset, been aware of the many volumes written by researchers on all aspects of black people's lives. Indeed without this insatiable interest in black people, the race relations industry would never have existed let alone flourished as it has done in the past ten years. Equally, black people are aware that the expansion in this race relations industry is not matched by any amelioration in the racism experienced by black people even in those areas researched. Why is this, and what is the point of doing this kind of research if it does nothing to redress the balance in the field of race? It becomes obvious from reading through some of the many volumes in the field of health that race relations research in the past avoided looking at institutional racism and concentrated instead on cultural and biological factors in explaining what are clearly the effects of racism and class oppression. As the Black Health Workers and Patients Group observed, black people too have been drawn into the distortion of such facts:

> 'A few black academics have been co-opted into institutions to do
> research into race-relations under the myth of scientific neutrality.
> These black people may believe that they are doing valuable work
> which will enhance race relations in this country. In fact they are

producing the raw material which will be processed by the race "experts" and used as the basis of racist social policy.'[39]

In the field of race relations there is just no room for 'neutrality'. The only meaningful approach is action research.

## 3. Action Research

Town has described action research as:

'a process whereby in a given problem area research is undertaken to specify the dimensions of the problem in its particular context; on the basis of this evidence a possible solution is formulated, and is translated into action with a view to solving the problem; research is then used to evaluate the effectiveness of the action taken. In this way action research may appear to be challenging the application of social science to the solution of social problems, by combining the knowledge and research techniques of social science both to discover solutions and to provide scientific evidence of their efficacy.'[40]

The history of action research goes back to the early 1950s with the Tavistock Institute and the Glacier Metals Project in which the concern of researchers was with the work-group relationships as well as management-worker relationships in the organisation under study. The main objective of action research in these projects was to improve the working of the organisation.

In the late 1960s and early 1970s the notion of action research was applied in the field of social problems and policy formation in the areas of war against poverty in the United States and in Britain, in Education Priority Areas as well as in Community Development Projects.[41] In all these projects the aim was to use research findings to stimulate action which was in turn a subject for research in terms of evaluating the changes emanating from that action. Such an approach is useful in that it makes research findings directly and immediately available for action whilst at the same time helping to distance social science from:

'the dubious "smash and grab" image of research where researchers study a situation for their own purpose and depart with the vague promise that all will be revealed when the research report is (finally) published.'[42]

Despite its radical approach, however, action research as applied in the above projects had still to contend with the problems inherent in

41

the distinction between 'action' and 'research' not only in principle but also in the geographical siting and responsibility. Those responsible for action in the case of the Community Development Projects, for example, were based in the Home Office or in Local Government departments and those responsible for research were in higher education institutions. As Ben-Tovim *et al* point out such a division creates problems among which are poor co-ordination, conflict of interest and a 'failure of action research to consider the political context and implications of the programme of action'.[43] The authors suggest that such difficulties can, however, be overcome through:

> 'the abandonment of any formal division between research and action responsibilities so that there is no institutionalised differentiation between the researcher or research team and the activist or action team.'[44]

They advocate a fusion of role in which the researcher is also the activist. This combination of role implies two very important responsibilities which are crucial in the field of race relations research. First, part of the research process would be concerned with the ways in which the products of research can be used as a form of intervention at a political level locally, nationally and internationally:

> 'For research purposes the process of implementation would be conceived not as an after-thought coming at the end of the research report with a list of recommendations uttered into a political vacuum, as is normally the case, but rather the implementation process would itself be an object of investigation to be integrally bound up with whatever other form the research might take.'[45]

Secondly, the fusion of role means that the researcher/activist has to have knowledge of those organisations concerned with political change. These will include statutory agencies responsible for policy implementation as well as bodies campaigning for such changes. Such an analysis is crucial because:

> 'Effective intervention requires a full understanding of the ideology, structure and functioning of these agencies, as well as the preparedness to inject the products of social science into the political and policy process in a variety of different forms and levels, to mesh in with the complexity of the process by which political decisions and policy implementation actually occur.'[46]

Action research, however, is not without its critics. It has been strongly argued that attempts to effect policy changes and practices tend to be pragmatic and reformist and thus tend to compromise radical change. In his review of 'The Racial Politics of Health' for example, Sashidharan expresses doubts about the usefulness of resorting to 'pressure group politics' at a local level. Those involved, he argues:

> 'may eventually succeed in changing the practice and delivery of health care in Merseyside by such approaches, but in doing so the case for radical change (i.e. for not accepting the constraints imposed by prevailing ideas about illness, disability or patients) is likely to be compromised in favour of reformist changes like more community care, less authoritarian attitudes etc.'[47]

This was also the stand taken by the Militant Tendency who controlled the City Council in Liverpool between 1983 and 1987. Suggestions to focus on specific areas of racist and sexist oppression at a local level tended to be rejected on the ground that they militated against the united support for the working class in their struggle which was seen to be singular and paramount. That capitalism is a negative force which is largely responsible for the present forms of racist, sexist and classist oppression is not here in question. Nor is the urgent need to find ways to create a more equal, just and fair alternative. What is in question however, is whether or not it is possible to find a mechanism to achieve such a society which can be sustained for an enduring period. Various suggestions have, of course, been made over the years: Lenin's 'smash the state apparatus' was tried in Cuba: the armed struggle has been attempted in Angola, Zimbabwe, and Mozambique. But what methods exist which would realistically provide the means to achieve radical yet enduring changes in Britain which would create a fairer, more equal and just society for all?

The action research approach is not put forward as a blue print for radical change but as a possible starting point in which group pressure politics can play an important role. First, group pressure politics are immediately concerned with life experiences as they affect people now, and that in the field of health means current racist practices in employment and delivery of services. If group pressure at this level actually achieves positive changes then those participating, seeing the results of their action, may be encouraged to take their fight further afield into other areas of life. In other words there is meaning in taking up a fight, a meaning relevant to people's lives now instead of the promises of hereafter socialism. This is not a compromise of long-term socialist struggles but rather a firm foundation for a fight for socialism. Group pressure politics are therefore not in themselves reformist. The question of whether group pressure politics remain purely reformist or are a starting point for a socialist struggle is dependent on the ways in which the ideas, aims and objectives of the participants involved develop and the extent to which participants envisage their future.

Secondly, through participation, group pressure politics are an effective form of the conscientisation which is both pragmatically and ideologically necessary in a successful fight for socialism. There cannot be a vanguard without people to lead, and in general people would be happy if they are led by leaders whose views and ideas they share. It is not enough to tell people that socialism will be good for them. They must discover for themselves that the change will be good for them, and they can only do so if they have full participation in all the processes which will be involved in bringing about that change: thinking, discussion, decision, planning and action. Pressure groups at local level, depending on how they are organised, can serve as micro units in which participants can re-learn the expertise of democratic involvement from which they have been excluded, which should be the hallmark of socialism. Without these preparatory stages socialism, like capitalism, will be an imposition by the vanguard which believes 'it is good for the people'. Group pressure politics at the local level do not necessarily compromise any long-term struggle for better health care in particular or socialism in general.

Thirdly, action research provides an opportunity for black people to share their experiences of racism and enables them to realise that it is the system and not them themselves that is to blame. Finally, action research provides some conscientisation of those in positions of power who are forced to think about the issues involved in racism even if it is to defend their policies. No apologies are made therefore and there are no dilemmas experienced through involvement in action research or in taking part in 'group pressure politics'. The dilemma arises not from the approach adopted but from the fact of being a black researcher.

Researchers and academics in general in universities belong to a very small group of privileged people in society. As a researcher you obtain a grant, admittedly not a lot of money, but still more than very many people who are unemployed have. If the research is successfully completed you are awarded a further degree which puts you in a better position for employment. If out of that research you produce a book your name becomes known and you get invited to seminars, conferences and discussion groups as an expert on your subject. If you are lucky you might get a well-paid job because of your qualification. There is no doubt about the whole range of rewards that accrue to the researcher. This remains the case whether or not the research has been beneficial to those researched. In recognition of the foregoing how can black researchers defend themselves against the charge that in the field of race relations they, like their white colleagues, live off the backs of black people? It may be difficult to do so. However, the dilemma then is what to do? Do black researchers turn their backs on race issues and concern themselves, as Alistair McIntyre did, with a 'general theory of holes'[48] or something equally rivetting and important? Some black people do not think that they can do that either, and so the dilemma remains.

We now wish to turn to the areas in which action research has been put into practice in this project.

## References

33. Torkington, N. P. K., *The Racial Politics of Health, op. cit.*

34. Weber, M., *Methodology of the Social Service*, Free Press, 1949.

35. Ben-Tovim, G. *et al*, *Race Policy and Local Politics*, 1985.

36. Becker, H., *Sociological Work: Method and Substance*, Aldine, 1970, p. 123.

37. Bulmer, M. (ed.), *Social Policy Research*, The Macmillan Press Ltd, 1978.

38. Ben-Tovim, G. *et al*, *op cit*, 1985.

39. Black Health Workers and Patients Group, *Black Health Bulletin*, September 1982, pp. 8–9.

40. Town, S. W., 'Action Research and Social Policy: British Experience', in Bulmer, M. (ed.), *op cit*, p. 161.

41. Ben-Tovim, G., *op cit*, 1985.

42. Town, S. W., *op cit*, p. 166.

43. Ben-Tovim, G., *op cit*, 1985.

44. Ibid.

45. Ibid.

46. Ibid.

47. Sashidharan, S. P., *Radical Community Care: Race and Health*, Baywood Publishing Company, 1983, p. 70.

48. Quoted in Bulmer, M. (ed.), *op cit*, pp. 20–21.

# Part Two
# **Consultative Papers**

This section is composed of six separate working papers produced in the course of the Project. The first is a review of the literature on black people and high blood pressure. The second covers the screening for blood pressure and diabetes; the third is on the Somali Community, the fourth looks at the poor up-take of hospital services by racial minority elderly people, the fifth is on the Interpreting Service and the last is on Mental Health.

# Black People and High Blood Pressure

High blood pressure or hypertension has, in recent years, become a topical area for discussion in medical circles as well as in medical journals. Central to the debate is the failure of doctors and the Health Service in general to treat the problem with the seriousness it deserves. Before we discuss the debate around this issue, it is necessary to look at the existing literature.

In 1984, an article in *The Lancet* pointed to a study which showed that high blood pressure:

> 'had not been recognised before the final illness in 27% of people, had been recognised but not treated in 20% and had been treated but not controlled in 51%.'[1]

In America it is estimated that as many as 35 million people have definite high blood pressure, 50% of whom are undiagnosed and only 10% getting adequate treatment. A further 25 million people are thought to be borderline hypertensives.[2]

There is consensus, however, about the position of black people in relation to hypertension. Most of the literature in this area suggests that black people, and in particular men, tend to have higher levels of blood pressure than do their white counterparts and that they suffer more from the consequences of that high blood pressure. Again *The Lancet* makes this point clear:

> 'and as well as having a higher blood pressure, the American Black person seems more susceptible to the consequences of hypertension: thus hypertensive vascular disease (strokes, memory loss, confusion etc.,) is even more common in the Black population than would be predicted from the increased prevalence of hypertension.'[3]

In the United States of America, Hosten points out, black people have high blood pressure compared with the general population.[4] In Johannesburg, South Africa, the number one killer among black adults is not malnutrition nor infection but high blood pressure.[5] This observation has been confirmed in our own discussion with black doctors and nurses working in South African hospitals who point out that the problem of hypertension and its related consequences, in particular stroke, is now affecting a large section of the black population.[6]

If there is agreement about the fact that black people tend to have a greater incidence of high blood pressure than do white people, there is no consensus about the reasons for that observed difference. One school of thought suggests that the problem may be genetically engineered. Some researchers have reported a correlation between the frequency of specific genes found in black people and levels of blood pressure.[7] For Boyle the frequency of the genes is reflected in the blackness of skin and in his study of black people in Charleston, South Carolina, he reported to have found a correlation between colour and elevated blood pressure.[8]

Further studies suggesting a genetic dimension in hypertension are cited in Hosten's work.[9] The problem that has been isolated as having a tendency to run in families is essential hypertension. Seedat, who reports having difficulties in getting a reliable family history among his black patients in South Africa, nevertheless claims to have found a positive family history of hypertension in 9% of his cases.[10]

The genetic argument has been extended to explain physiological aspects of hypertension. Within this school of thought it is suggested that black people have a genetic predisposition not to excrete as much sodium as do white people.[11] This means that a given amount of salt which would be normally harmless when ingested by a white individual is likely to produce hypertension when eaten by a black person. Another hypothesis related to the sodium theory suggests that:

'the black is innately more thrifty with sodium than the white as a consequence of an evolutionary history in a sweating, salt-poor tropical climate, compared to the white's descent from ancestors living in a more frigid, salt-replete environment.'[12]

This also suggests that if such black people were to live in the 'frigid salt-replete' areas they would have problems with high blood pressure. Langford rightly dismisses this hypothesis since there is no adequate data on which to base such a conclusion.

Other researchers in this area have found that black people tend to have a suppressed plasma renin activity and this leads to low renin hypertension.[13] Renin is a substance produced in the kidneys and it is believed to be involved in the maintenance and control of blood pressure. In addition, it is suggested, black people have a higher relative plasma volume when compared with whites.[14]

Explanations of high blood pressure among black people become not only problematic but extremely dangerous when rooted in genetic factors. They are dangerous because they introduce the element of 'naturalness'. This will invariably lead some health professionals to accept higher levels of blood pressure as normal when they occur in black people, a rationale for doing nothing to combat the problem. This has been discussed in the course of this Project with some GPs who were aware that black people tend to have high blood pressure but wondered if they 'necessarily suffer in consequence'. The frightening aspect of such ignorance lies in the fact that levels of high blood pressure which have little effect when occurring in white people are likely to have disastrous consequences when affecting black people.[15] The work of Moriyama *et al* also shows that black people are more likely than white people to die from hypertension related diseases in the United States of America.[16] Citing the 1973 Vital Statistics of the United States, Gillum writes:

> 'Of special interest is the fact that between the ages of 35 to 54 years, blacks died six to 10 times as frequently from hypertensive disease according to 1973 statistics, an excess far out of proportion to the approximate two times excess of prevalence of hypertension in blacks.'[17]

This suggests to us that more notice should be taken when a black person presents with high blood pressure, that more and not less vigorous investigation and monitoring should be undertaken in the black community if such disasters are to be avoided.

A further dangerous consequence of genetic explanations is that they invariably locate the problem within the individual. The tendency that follows is to encourage the individual to adopt a particular 'life-style' in order to accommodate the abnormal gene and therefore minimize its bad effect. That way of perceiving the problem is likely to slow down, if not totally discourage, the process of searching for other possible causes outside the individual. As Watkins points out:

> '. . . such emphasis on the role of the individual in disease prevention increases the risk that policy-makers will fail to recognize the intricate connections between socio-economic status and health enhancing behaviours and will resort to "blaming the victim".'[18]

Even when socio-economic factors are recognized and acknowledged the tendency is still to minimise their significance either by confining them to those areas in which the individual remains the one holding the key to the solution of the problem or by choosing not to look at the wider social, political and economic factors outside the individual when conducting research. Genetic explanations are attractive. They locate the problem within the individual. In that way society, within which that individual is situated, is vindicated and seen not to be implicated in the production of the problem under review. These explanations fit neatly into quantitative statistical data and therefore can be presented with the objectivity of 'scientific research'. But significant environmental factors are rooted in the way the structure of society is organized. The effect they have on the individual cannot always be measured in statistical terms. That is not very attractive to statistically-minded researchers. But what is more important is that their inclusion in the line of inquiry would call for different forms of solutions, the application of which would have as a starting point the questioning of the very basic structure of society.

Another problem with genetic explanations is introduced by the inconsistencies reflected in the different results of studies of high blood pressure presented to us. Genetically determined health problems should by their very nature remain a given, irrespective of short-term changes in environment. The environment may at best ameliorate or at worst exacerbate the condition, but its presence cannot be eliminated by such changes. This is certainly the situation in the case of sickle cell. Geneticists state that the muted sickle gene is going to remain in our blood for thousands of years to come irrespective of the Diaspora. But this does not appear to be the case with high blood pressure.

In their study of the Xhosa people in South Africa, Sever *et al* found that high blood pressure was a problem with those people who had become urban dwellers. Among the 133 rural people, blood pressure rose little with age; and this was in contrast to the 141 urban dwellers in whom there was a steep rise with age.[19]

Sever *et al* touch on environmental factors implicated in their findings. The first factor is weight. In general 'Urban blacks were heavier and fatter than tribal blacks'.[20] But it was the urban black women who were heavier and more obese than white men and women. The authors also tell us that 'urban black men are the least obese' and yet up to the age of 40 years they had the highest blood pressure out of all the four groups. The other factor is salt. But salt is dismissed because it was equally available and used by both tribal and urban groups. Because of this the authors are not certain if dietary salt can be seen as a causal factor.

From their study Sever *et al* concluded that:

'. . . in more unsophisticated and tribal environments blood pressures are lower, do not rise with age and hypertension is uncommon. Thus environmental factors associated with urbanisation or acculturation may play an important role in blood pressure elevation in the black.'[21]

Perhaps more interesting are the environmental factors that the researchers engaged in a study of black people under apartheid in South Africa excluded from the line of their inquiry:

'The possible role of psychosocial and economic factors in the rise in arterial pressure in urban dwellers is another attractive hypothesis, but one which this study was not designed to investigate.'[22]

One wonders why this area, so crucial in the lives of black people in South Africa, was not investigated. Another study which contrasted the levels of blood pressure between black rural and urban dwellers was conducted by Miall *et al* in Jamaica.[23] Their findings negate the conclusions of Sever *et al* in which urbanisation or acculturation were seen to be playing an important role in the development of high blood pressure. In the Jamaican study it was the rural women of the Lawrence Tavern Village who suffered from hypertension. The authors report that the conditions of existence for these women:

'were such that one would expect a low prevalence of those diseases which are characteristically associated with high living standard.'[24]

And yet it was in this 'unsophisticated' environment that severe hypertension among women was more common and was associated with cerebro-vascular accidents. Nine out of twelve women in the rural group who had a cerebrovascular complication had diastolic pressures exceeding 110 mm Hg as opposed to one out of five urban women in this category.

It is neither possible nor productive in the context of this work to go through all the literature in order to show the problems inherent in explanations which draw heavily on genetic factors or are selective in their use of environmental factors. But before reporting the findings of the screening which was undertaken for the Project, another school of thought is briefly considered – that which puts forward strongly the structural environmental factors which might be implicated in elevated levels of blood pressure among black people.

In his work Gillum acknowledges the possible role played by genetic factors, personal characteristics, renal physiology, endocrine factors and autonomic nervous system function as well as various environmental factors in the elevation of blood pressure among black people. The structural position of black people in the racist society is an area to which Gillum draws the attention of those who are searching for possible causes of the problem.

> 'Blacks are more frequently exposed to conditions of poverty, low occupational and educational status and high levels of socio-ecologic stress, all of which are related to the prevalence of hypertension in both blacks and whites. In addition, racial discrimination has long been postulated to be a stress creating factor for blacks in the United States which might play a role in the pathogenesis of essential hypertension.'[25]

Langford draws attention to a study of school children in America in which rural white boys had higher systolic pressure when compared with urban black children from an upper socio-economic group. Another example of the effect of environmental factors on blood pressure is reflected in the fact that in general both black and white people living in the North have lower blood pressures compared to those living in the South and those inhabiting the far West probably have lower pressures than those living in the other two areas.[26] From these findings Langford suggests that the question of genetic black-white differences may indeed be impossible to address until the nature of these environmental forces was identified and quantified.

In their work Keil et al argue against the study carried out by Boyle in Charleston, South Carolina in which he linked elevated blood pressure to genetic factors as manifested in skin colour. They stress social class and the life-style associated with it. For the black population in Charleston that life-style included:

> 'exposure to infectious diseases, pollutants, climatic factors, diet, stress generated by concern for personal safety, crowding, lack of life's necessities, or even sudden affluence. Finally, one must consider the social and psychological restraints imposed on Blacks.'[27]

An editorial in the *American Journal of Public Health* picked up the skin colour blood pressure theme in 1978 and argued that skin colour may in fact be an indicator of psychosocial processes. They based their reasoning on the historical perspective concerning skin colour and status:

> 'Chronic elevations of blood pressure in human populations may be related in part to struggles – under conditions of great uncertainty – to acquire sufficient economic and social resources to 'control' one's environment;
>
> These struggles are less intense or, at least, often rewarded for persons of higher social status;
>
> In industrialized, male-oriented and dominated societies, the struggle for environmental mastery has been led by males;
>
> In color conscious societies, access to economic and social resources is greatly influenced by one's skin color;
>
> In American society, darker skin black men, and those dependent on them for survival – more than most other sub-groups – have been denied full access to these resources, with the result that a satisfactory degree of environmental control is rarely achieved.'[28]

In Mokhobo's view an area which deserves special scrutiny is diet and the area he is particularly concerned about is potassium depletion. In rural African areas where black people live the main diet consists of starch with a low intake of proteins and vegetables. Mokhobo dismisses tension during the process of acculturation as a cause of hypertension. He argues that:

> 'tension is a universal phenomenon in all societies and therefore cannot be readily invoked to explain the emergence of hypertension among Blacks.'[29]

Mokhobo also finds the role of genetic mechanism and inbreeding unacceptable as an explanation of elevated blood pressure among black people. For him chronic potassium deficiency seems the most likely explanation for the phenomenon.

The role of potassium in the causation of high blood pressure among black people in Western societies has also been stressed by other writers on the subject. Gillum dismisses differential sodium intake on the ground that many studies done in America found no difference in black and white sodium intake.[30] The difference, according to a study by Langford *et al*, is in the intake of potassium and calcium. Black people, the study showed, have a lower intake of these ingredients in their food compared to white people. The presence of both electrolytes in the blood stream have been shown to promote the excretion of sodium.[31] Food which is rich in potassium and calcium is expensive, hence the link made by some writers between poverty (a phenomenon experienced by most black people) and higher levels of blood pressure among black people.

Working on this area Gillum says:

> 'Thus a culturally and economically determined relative deficiency of dietary potassium and calcium among blacks has been postulated to contribute to the higher blood pressures and occurrence of hypertension observed among blacks as compared to whites.'[32]

From the above discussion it is obvious that the whole area of high blood pressure in relation to black people is a complex one. Genetic factors are implicated. But as we have argued earlier an over-emphasis on this aspect of the problem runs the risk of minimizing the role of the environment. Even when there appears to be a clear case of genetic determinism as reflected in positive family history of hypertension, it is as well to remember that 'family members are usually exposed to the same environmental factors'.[33] Similarly, genes cannot be given priority in explaining differences of blood pressure between black and white people because as the *Lancet* pointed out:

> 'Racial differences are almost always associated with differences in social environment and the blood circulation is notoriously susceptible to such environmental influences.'[34]

It is indeed possible that what presents as a genetic problem is environmental in origin.

The immediate concern of this Project is not to resolve the controversy in the causation of high blood pressure in black people. Whatever its causes, the major point is that there is a problem and the question is what can be done about it. For a variety of reasons there is no simple answer to that question.

Firstly, an early rise in blood pressure can only be detected through screening and to date there are very few health centres and surgeries which provide this service as a matter of course. Even if these centres did provide such a service they would only succeed in catering for people who do consult them for other health matters. From our discussion with some local G.P.'s we know this group is mainly composed of women. Black men, who are the main target for high blood pressure, would on the whole be excluded.

Secondly there is no agreement among doctors as to what constitutes high blood pressure and at what level treatment would be commenced. The World Health Organisation's definition of hypertension is blood pressure which is equal or greater than 160/95 mm Hg or below that only if the person is receiving treatment.[35] A study of physicians' attitudes conducted by Bucknall et al shows that very few doctors agree with this definition.[36] A significant number of doctors in this study would not treat systolic hypertension irrespective of the patient's age. For those who would have offered treatment, their decision would have been determined by the age of the patient. For the 30–49 age group treatment would have been recommended if systolic pressure was 151–160; 161–170 for the 50–59 age group and 180 + for the over 70 age group. Most doctors in the study recommended treatment with a rise in diastolic pressure in relation to age:

    91– 95 in the 30–49 year groups
    101–105 in the 50–69 year groups
    110 + in the over 70's group

A further complication in this area is introduced by the use of two end points in recording diastolic pressure: phase IV and phase V. According to the researchers if:

> 'two physicians agree to treat patients with diastolic pressures of 100 mm Hg and over, then the one who uses phase V will give a lifetime of treatment to 15% of his patients while the physician who uses phase IV will treat 25% of his patients. A difference of 10% in workload, drug costs, and patient inconvenience cannot be ignored so our study confirms that as diastolic anarchy is still with us therapeutic anarchy must also prevail.'[37]

As the authors point out it is indeed difficult to see how doctors can give clear guidance to their patients if they fail to recognise and resolve such major uncertainties in medicine itself. These divergent views make it impossible to transfer blood pressure readings from one doctor to the other or from trial results to practising physicians and, as the researchers suggest, the medical profession must put its house in order if any progress is to be made in tackling the problem of high blood pressure.

Thirdly, there is a question of whether or not treatment is beneficial to all patients who have elevated blood pressures. Wilcox and his associate have no doubts about the benefit of treatment in patients with malignant or accelerated phase hypertension.[38] But since the completion of nine clinical trials of the effects of reducing high blood pressure in which 50,000 patients participated, the authors are less sure about the benefits of treatment in people with non-accelerated hypertension. Although there were inadequacies in terms of criteria used, some of the trials showed that in some cases raised blood pressure often becomes normal with placebo treatment. In the Australian study, for example, 47% of the patients in the placebo group reached a diastolic pressure of less than 95 mm Hg within three years and most of them within the first four months. Similarly in the Medical Research Council (MRC) study about 40% of men and 45% of women in the control group had a reduced diastolic pressure of less than 90 mm Hg after one year. In the same study there were 60 strokes in the treated group and 109 in the placebo group. In the overall coronary event rate there was no significant difference between the treated group, 222 and the placebo group 234. From these results the MRC study concluded that:

> 'if 750 mildly hypertensive patients are given active anti-hypertensive drugs for one year, approximately one stroke will be prevented. This is an important but an infrequent benefit. Its achievement involved a substantial percentage of the patients in chronic side-effects, mostly but not all minor. It did not appear that treatment saved lives or that it substantially altered the overall risk of coronary heart disease. More than 95% of the control patients remained free of any cardio-vascular event during the trial.'[39]

The long-term side-effects for most of the patients include gout, impotence, lethargy and Raynaud's phenomenon.[40]

The information so far presented shows that there is no consensus on the causes of high blood pressure and there is also no agreement among the medical practitioners as to when and how to treat this condition. But whatever the different views, it is obvious that no choice can be made unless the level of blood pressure of the individual is known. It is for this reason that screening for blood pressure, in order to provide this information to both patient and doctor where possible, has been incorporated in the work of the Project. The different sessions of screening in various centres will now be discussed.

# References

1. Editorial, 'Towards a Better General Practice', *Lancet*, December 22/29 1984, p. 1436.

2. Hosten, Adrian O., 'Hypertension in Black and Other Populations: Environmental Factors and Approaches to Management', *Journal of the National Medical Association*, Vol. 72, No. 2, 1984.

3. Editorial, 'Hypertension in Blacks and Whites', *Lancet*, 12 July 1984, p. 73.

4. Hosten, Adrian O., *op cit*, 1980.

5. Seftel, H. C., 'Epidemiology of Hypertension in Developed and Developing Populations', *South African Medical Journal*, 53: 957–959, 1978.

6. Private communications with professionals involved in health care of black people in South Africa.

7. McLean, C. J., Adams, M. S., Leyshon, W. C., Workman, P. L., Reed, T. E., Gershowitz, H. and Wertramp, L. R., 'Genetics Studies on Hybrid Population III: Blood Pressure in an American Black Community', *American Journal of Human Genetics*, 26, 614, 1974.

8. Boyle, J. and E., 'Biological Patterns in Hypertension by Race, Sex, Body Weight and Skin Color', *Journal of the American Medical Association*, 213, 1637, 1970.

9. Hosten, Adrian O., *op cit*, 1980.

10. Seedat, Y. K., 'Genetic Factors in Hypertension', *South African Medical Journal*, 53: 960–964, 1978.

11. Luft, G. C., 'Differences in Response to Sodium Administration in Normotensive White and Black Subjects', *Journal of Laboratory and Clinical Medicine*, 90, 555, 1977.

12. Langford, H. G., 'Is Blood Pressure Different in Black People?', *Postgraduate Medical Journal*, 57, 749–754 (December), 1981.

13. Helmer, O. M. and Judson, W. E., 'Metabolic Studies on Hypertensive Patients with Suppressed Plasma Renin Activity not due to Hyperaldosteronism', *Circulation*, 38, 965, 1968.

14. Mitus, I. A., 'Racial Analysis of the Volume-Renin Relationship in Human Hypertension', *Archives of Internal Medicine*, 61: 208, 1964.

15. McDonough, J. R., Garrison, G. E. and Hames, C. G., 'Blood Pressure and Hypertensive Disease among Negroes and Whites', *Archives of Internal Medicine*, 61: 208, 1964. The HDFP Cooperative Groups: 'Sex and Race Differences in End Organ Damage among 10,940 Hypertensives', *American Journal of Cardiology*, 41: 402, 1978.

16. Moriyama, I., *Cardiovascular Disease in the United States*, Cambridge, Mass, Harvard University Press, p. 119, 1971.

17. Gillum, R. F., 'Pathophysiology of Hypertension in Blacks and Whites. A review of the Basis of Racial Blood Pressure Differences', *Hypertension*, Vol. 1, No. 5, September–October 1979.

18. Watkins, L. O., 'Preventing Cardiovascular Disease in Blacks: A Perspective', *Health and Medicine*, Spring 1985.

19. Sever, P. S., 'Racial Differences in Blood Pressure: Genetic and Environmental Factors', *Postgraduate Medical Journal*, 57, 755–759, December 1981.

20. Ibid, p. 61.

21. Ibid, pp. 60–61.

22. Ibid, p. 64.

23. Miall, W. E., Kass, E. H., Ling, G. and Stuart, K. L., 'Factors Influencing Arterial Pressure in the General Population in Jamaica', *British Medical Journal*, August 25 1962, pp. 497–506.

24. Ibid, p. 497.

25. Gillum, R. F., *op cit*, 1979, p. 473.

26. Langford, H. G., *op cit*, 1981.

27. Keil, Julian E., Tyroler, H. A., Sandifer, S. H.and Boyle, E., 'Hypertension: Effects of Social Class and Racial Admixture: The Results of a Cohort Study in the Black Population of Charleston, South Carolina', *American Journal of Public Health*, Vol. 67, No. 7, July 1977, p. 638.

28. Editorial, *American Journal of Public Health*, Vol. 68, No. 12, December 1978, p. 1172.

29. Mokhobo, K. P., 'Lifestyle and Disease: Aspects of Hypertension among Blacks', *S. A. Mediese Tydskrif*, 12 June 1982, p. 930.

30. Gillum, R. F., *op cit*, 1979.

31. Langford, H. G., 'Electrolytes and Hypertension', in Paul O. (ed.), *Epidemiology and Control of Hypertension*, New York Stratten Intercontinental Med Books, 1975.

32. Gillum, R. F., *op cit*, p. 473.

33. Hosten, A. O., *op cit*, p. 113.

34. Editorial, 'Hypertension in Blacks and Whites', *Lancet*, July 12 1980, p. 73.

35. Cruickshank, J. K., 'Vascular Disease in West Indian and White Diabetics in Britain and Jamaica', *Postgraduate Medical Journal*, 57, 766–768, December 1981.

36. Bucknall, C. A., Morris, G. K. and Mitchell, J. R. A., 'Physicians' Attitudes to Four Common Problems: Transient Ischaemic Attack and Angina Pectoris', *British Medical Journal*, Vol. 293, 20 September 1986.

37. Ibid, p. 741.

38. Wilcox, R. G., 'Treatment of High Blood Pressure: Should Clinical Practice be Based on Results of Clinical Trials?', *British Medical Journal*, Vol. 293, 16 August 1986.

39. M. R. C. Trial of Treatment of Mild Hypertension: Principal Results.

40. Wilcox *et al*, *op cit*.

Consultative Paper Two

# Screening in Health and Community Centres

## 1. Blood Pressure Screening in the Caribbean Centre

This was the first screening carried out in the community and to that extent it served as a pilot study for the researchers to test out the feasibility of screening in terms of people's reaction to it, the amount of work involved, the difficulties that might arise and the kind of questions to ask in relation to blood pressure.

### a. Methodology

The initial aim was to screen members of the Jamaican Association who generally meet in the Caribbean Centre on the first Sunday of every month. The Secretary of the Association was approached and arrangements were made for the researcher to meet the members and discuss the possibility of carrying out blood pressure screening. At the meeting, on the 6th April 1986, the aims and objectives of the whole Project were outlined to the members of the Association. The reasons why it was felt important to screen for blood pressure particularly among people of Afro-Caribbean origin were discussed with those present.

Among the participants were health professionals. An attempt was made to involve them actively in the Project. The suggestion was that the researcher would work with them as a team, but that they as members of that community would take over the screening as their own Project. They would write the report which would be published in their own health journal. The results of the screening would then be included in the final report of the Health and Race Project. There are many reasons why this idea was attractive.

The first and obvious one is personal interest. Working with health professionals would have eased the load of work. The second was to make the Project truly community based, not only in the geographical sense but on an ideological as well as practical level where black health professionals begin to use their expertise to promote health and discuss health issues in their own communities. The third was to encourage black health professionals to engage in action research and influence their professional organisation in implementing policies which acknowledge the specific health needs of black people. Many projects and publications on black health issues have been undertaken by white health professionals, and black health workers who are members of communities in question have been left in the background.

Although the idea, for the above reasons, was attractive, there remained an awareness that involving people in this way was nevertheless exploitative unless they received payment for the work they were doing. But discussion at that level was never reached because it became obvious from our discussion, after the main meeting, that none of the health workers would have time to be involved in the way suggested. They all agreed however that they would help out by taking blood pressures if time allowed and indeed some of them did help in the course of the screening.

The discussion with health professionals was very helpful. Questions were raised about the possibility of alarming people when levels of elevated blood pressure were found, the anxiety that would be caused by taking a person's blood pressure twice and the effect of that anxiety on the second reading. Questions were devised for the respondents and it was decided to screen once a month (first Sunday when members meet) for six months to see if there was any change in the individual's blood pressure in that time. Unfortunately pressure of work in other areas of the Project made it difficult to sustain screening for this period, and it had to be stopped after three months.

The actual screening started on the 4th May 1986. A table and a chair were placed at the back of the meeting room and members had their blood pressure taken before the meeting started. As soon as the meeting started the researcher moved out into the main foyer of the Centre and the rest of the people who came in for social reasons were asked if they would like to have their blood pressure measured. Some people were not interested. Others were keen and wanted more discussion, not only on blood pressure but on other health issues as well.

### b. The Results of Screening

The respondents were predominantly men. The total number screened was 37 and only two were women. The health workers who were women did not have their blood pressure taken because they knew that it was normal. Most respondents were from the Caribbean, only eight were Liverpool born black people and one of them was a woman. Most Afro-Caribbean respondents fell in the 40–70 age category.

**Table 2   Afro-Caribbean Respondents**

| Age | No. of People |
|-----|---------------|
| 30–39 years | 1 |
| 40–49 years | 7 |
| 50–59 years | 11 |
| 60–69 years | 6 |
| Over 70 years | 4 |
| | 29 |

By contrast the Liverpool born black people were younger, most of them less than 20 years old. This came about as a result of an enthusiastic respondent who went to the Sports Centre and invited young black children to come and have their blood pressure checked.

**Table 3   Liverpool-Born Black Respondents**

| Age | No. of People |
|-----|---------------|
| 13 years | 1 |
| 15 years | 1 |
| 17 years | 1 |
| 19 years | 2 |
| 20–30 years | 2 |
| 40–50 years | 1 |
| | 8 |

Most of the people screened had diastolic pressures which were less than 95 mm Hg. Since most doctors would be less concerned about this group only the results of the readings which were at or above this level are given here.

Those respondents who did not know that they had elevated blood pressure were advised to see their General Practitioner and ask for a further blood pressure check. The role of diet, smoking, weight and

### Table 4   Screening Results

| Age | Sex | May | June | July | Remarks on Treatment |
|-----|-----|-----|------|------|----------------------|
| 70 | M | 168/100 | 140/95 | — | |
| 40–50 | M | 150/110 | — | — | Didn't know he had high BP. |
| 40–50 | M | 136/100 | 130/98 | 134/90 | Didn't know. |
| 50–60 | M | 130/100 | 148/116 | — | Didn't know. |
| 60–70 | M | 130/100 | — | — | Didn't know. |
| Over 70 | M | 130/100 | — | — | Didn't know. |
| 50–60 | M | 144/108 | — | — | His doctor knows but is not on treatment. |
| Over 70 | M | 210/100 | — | — | Had been on doctor's treatment but now trying homeopathy. |
| 60–70 | M | 140/98 | — | — | On treatment. |
| 60–70 | M | 150/118 | — | — | Didn't know. |
| 60–70 | M | 170/110 | — | — | On treatment but not taking medication regularly. |

exercise in the control of high blood pressure was discussed with individuals who had high readings. With the exception of one person all those on treatment had been taking medication regularly. All had been advised by their doctors to lose weight, cut down on salt intake and smoking and take regular exercise.

Those involved in this Project are in no position to suggest whether or not people with that level of blood pressure should be put on medication. That decision lies with their doctors. What is maintained, however, is that it is important for the doctor and the patient to know what the situation is. A balance has to be reached between the side-effects of medication and a possibility of hypertensive complications which some believe could occur in black people even if they only have small diastolic increases. That area of discussion must concern both doctor and patient. But that discussion cannot even begin if there is no screening, the results of which would inform both parties that there is a problem to be tackled.

Screening for high blood pressure and diabetes has continued both in the Community Centres and in Health Centres. Screening sessions have been held in Abercromby Health Centre, Hindu Community

Centre, Merseyside Community Relations Council, the Somali Centre, the Pakistan Centre and Princes Park Health Centre.

## 2. Screening in Health Centres: Methodology

Abercromby and Princes Park Health Centres are both in the Liverpool 8 area where most racial minorities live. It was felt therefore that it was important to set up a Screening Project in both Centres in order to contact as many racial minorities as possible. It was also important to include white patients who may have undetected high blood pressure and diabetes. The inclusion of white patients in the sample was to provide a health check service to this group as well as to provide an opportunity to have a control group in the Screening Project.

Prior to screening, discussions were held with doctors, administrators, receptionists and clerks in Abercromby and Princes Park Health Centres. The doctors welcomed the proposal provided it had the approval and support of the local Medical Committee. Doctors in Princes Park Health Centre felt that the Screening Project provided an opportunity to find out if the primary health care service that was being provided was adequate and acceptable to patients. It was suggested that the questionnaire should be extended to include a 'women only' section. It was also felt that urine testing was not accurate in detecting early diabetes and therefore blood sugar screening was suggested. The doctors offered to train the researcher, who was herself a trained nurse, in the procedure of blood sugar screening using disposable needles to ensure non-contamination of both patient and researcher. The health check offered to patients therefore included blood pressure, urine testing, blood sugar testing, weight, height, a questionnaire and a general discussion on health related factors such as smoking, diet, alcohol, exercise and any other health topic on which a patient wanted information. The team in the Project included neighbourhood health workers who had been previously trained in taking blood pressure, urine testing, weight and height checking and who in the course of their work became familiar with and gained knowledge of a variety of health topics.

c

## 3. Screening in Abercromby Health Centre

In Abercromby Health Centre there are two independent group practices, each with a senior partner. The initial discussions were with each of the senior partners and later with their respective partners.

A week before screening notices were posted in the Centre informing patients about the screening which was to be conducted in one of the consulting rooms currently used by the Health and Race Project. Doctors were sent copies of the questionnaire and asked for their approval before it was administered to their patients. The questionnaire, however, created some confusion as doctors mistakenly linked it to a previous survey specifically on women's preference for female doctors which had been submitted earlier by the Liverpool (Central & Southern) Community Health Council and had been rejected by one group practice in the Centre. After some discussion the confusion was resolved but there was still some reluctance to have the questionnaire administered on three grounds:

(a) asking patients about preferences concerning doctors might create ill-feelings and tension between doctor and patient.

(b) doctors should inform their patients about other services in the area which relate to women e.g. cytology, Well Women Clinics and Family Planning Clinics.

(c) that doctors had worked in the area for a long time and had good relationships with the community and with racial minorities and they did not want any problems, and there would be problems if the researchers started asking questions.

One group practice did not want its patients to be asked any questions and did not want researchers to tell patients in the waiting room about screening as the doctors were going to tell them about this service during consultation. The other group practice agreed to the questionnaire provided the section on 'women only' was deleted, and also agreed that researchers could talk to patients in the waiting room about the Project. This lack of uniformity inevitably led to problems which will be dealt with later in the general discussion. The original questionnaire was adapted to conform to the doctors' demands in this centre.

### a. The Results of the Screening

Because of other commitments only two weeks of screening covering morning sessions only from 9.30 a.m.–1.00 p.m. could be offered by the researchers. In that period 67 patients were screened, some of whom were not patients in the Health Centre. They came either independently or with relatives after hearing about the screening facility.

Table 5   Nationality of People Screened

| Nationality | Male | Female |
|---|---|---|
| African | 2 | 2 |
| British Black | 6 | 15 |
| British White | 18 | 17 |
| Chinese | 0 | 0 |
| West Indian | 4 | 1 |
| South Asian | 1 | 1 |
| Total | 31 | 36 |

The age of participants ranged from 17 years to 74 years. Most people screened had a diastolic pressure of less than 95 mm Hg and since there is less concern about people in this category the results that will be shown in this report will be for those with diastolic pressure above 95 mm Hg or those below it but on treatment. Many people felt that giving a urine specimen was a cumbersome process and declined to do so whilst others declined to have a blood sugar test. All the tests were offered on a voluntary basis and patients were not pressurised to accept any part of the screening. The blood sugar results and the urine test results shown here are those above the accepted average of normality. The procedures involved in screening were done in the presence of the patient who was shown how the tests were done and was given enough time and encouragement to ask questions.

As Table 6 shows, not many people had high blood pressure or diabetes. One African male had a blood pressure of 170/120 and was on treatment. There was one West Indian woman with a blood pressure of 178/102 and she too was on treatment. Out of 18 British White males, three had a blood pressure of 170/110, 170/110 and 150/90 respectively and all of them were on treatment. One of them had had a stroke and had given up smoking but the other two were non-smokers and non-drinkers. There was one British White female aged 74 who had a blood pressure of 200/100 and was not on treatment. Although a diastolic pressure of 100 mm Hg may be accepted

**Table 6  Screening Results**

| Nationality | Sex | Age | B.P. | Urine | Bl. Sugar | Smoking | Alcohol | Comments |
|---|---|---|---|---|---|---|---|---|
| African | M | middle aged (not given) | 170/120 | neg. | n/d | N/S | N/D | On treatment for high blood pressure |
| W. Indian | F | 56 | 178/102 | n/d | 4.4 | N/S | N/D | On treatment for high blood pressure |
| British W | M | 68 | 170/110 | n/d | n/d | N/S | N/D | On treatment for high blood pressure |
| British W | M | 65 | 170/110 | n/d | n/d | given up | N/D | On treatment for high blood pressure Had had a stroke |
| British W | M | 65 | 150/90 | neg. | n/d | N/S | N/D | On treatment for high blood pressure |
| British W | M | 66 | 156/90 | — | 10 | N/S | N/D | Not on treatment for diabetes |
| British W | F | 74 | 200/100 | n/d | 2.2 | S | Drinks moderate | Not on treatment for high blood pressure |
| British W | F | 59 | 162/70 | neg. | 10 | S | Drinks moderate | On treatment for diabetes |

KEY:  M = Male  F = Female  W = White  n/d = not done  N/S = Non-Smoker  S = Smoker  N/D = Non-Drinker  neg. = negative as normal at her age it was felt that a systolic pressure of 200 mm Hg might have been a bit high even at such an age.

There was only one patient, a British White female, who had diabetes and was on treatment. She had a blood sugar of 10. One British White man had blood sugar of 10 with a large amount of sugar in his urine but was not on treatment. The results of screening were given to the doctors in the Centre.

Obviously the number of people who took part in the Abercromby Health Centre Screening Project is low and does not allow general conclusions to be drawn. But it is thought noteworthy that 22% of Afro-Caribbeans had high blood pressure and only 11.4% of white people suffered from this condition.

### b. General Discussion

Abercromby was the first Health Centre in which screening was carried out and therefore it served as a pilot study, and obviously there were lessons to be learned. It was perhaps inevitable that tension would arise between researchers who were viewed as outsiders with perhaps a potential to disrupt the normal running of the Centre. There was indeed an occasion when a patient came for screening and the receptionist had to come and ask him to go for his consultation with the doctor or he would lose his appointment time. But once it was explained to patients that they had to see the doctor first, such incidents did not re-occur.

One group practice did not want the researcher to talk to patients about the screening project in the waiting room as the notices were believed to be enough to inform patients about the service and the doctors were themselves going to inform patients during consultation. The problem here is that not many people take notice of posters unless someone draws their attention to them and the doctors also admitted later that they had not enough time to be telling patients about the screening. In the two weeks of the screening, doctors in the morning sessions were consulted by approximately 493 patients and of these only 46 were tested for this research.

It was not anticipated that all patients would want to be screened but it was still felt that all patients should know about the availability of the service.

All the patients who did come to see us were very interested in the Screening Project and felt that general health checks should be available as part of health provision in primary health care. Some patients wanted to talk about their lives in general and in particular the stresses they faced. Two young men felt that very little was done in terms of health promotion and preventative health care for men and were very keen on the idea of a Well Man Clinic. One of the doctors in the Health Centre was also interested in a Well Man Clinic and it is hoped to have further discussion on this topic.

In two weeks more people living in the area had heard about the Screening Project and people who were not consulting the doctors were coming in to be screened. Some were not even patients of the Centre. Even after the screening finished the researchers were informed by receptionists that more people came asking to be tested.

## 4. Screening in Princess Park Health Centre

After the screening sessions in Abercromby Health Centre the researchers reported the results to the Health and Race Project Steering Committee. Some medical members of the Committee expressed concern about the blood sugar tests even though they had been carried out by a trained nurse with the approval of the doctors and with the permission of patients. There was a suggestion that the Medical Ethical Committee should have been approached for its approval. Although most members of the Committee did not follow this view, it was eventually agreed that since this concern had been raised it was advisable to discontinue blood sugar testing in future screening sessions. At Princess Park Health Centre, therefore, only urine testing was offered even though doctors in this centre were particularly keen to have blood sugar testing done. But urine testing was not only inconvenient but also embarrassing for patients since they had to walk quite a distance from the toilets to bring their urine specimen to the screening room. Many patients declined the offer and this procedure was eventually excluded from the screening.

### a. The Results of the Screening

Since there was growing pressure from other areas of Project work, even less time was spent in this centre. As the following table shows, only 40 patients were screened.

The ages of those screened varied between 19 and 74 years with 70% in the 20–40 year band. Thirty-eight of the patients had normal blood pressure. One, a 66 year old white woman, had a pressure of 220/118. Neither her doctors nor the patient were aware of this fact before screening and the patient reported no ill-effects to her health. The other patient, a 65 year old white woman, told researchers that

**Table 7  Nationality of People Screened in Princess Park Health Centre**

| Nationality | Male | Female |
|---|---|---|
| African | 1 | 1 |
| British Black | 1 | 5 |
| British White | 14 | 18 |
| Chinese | 0 | 0 |
| Caribbean | 0 | 0 |
| South Asian | 0 | 0 |
| Total | 16 | 24 |

she had high blood pressure. She was not on treatment and when screened the pressure was 135/75.

### b. The Results of the Questionnaire

In Princess Park Health Centre doctors had asked that a questionnaire be included as part of the screening process. The questionnaire sought to elicit information on a number of areas: the length of time patients had been registered with the Centre; how many times in the last two years they had consulted their doctor; whether or not their blood pressure had been measured in the last two years; whether or not they smoked; if any of their first degree relatives had died or suffered from cardio-vascular diseases or diabetes; and finally they were asked to comment on the service they received from the Centre. General questions were asked in the first part of the questionnaire. The second part was for 'women only' and it addressed the area of Well-Woman clinics. For clarity, the results of the general question-naire will be reported first from each of the four groups: black women, black men, white women and white men. The results of the Well-Woman questionnaire will be presented in table form.

### c. Black Women – Results of General Questionnaire

On the length of time registered with the Centre, one woman had only been a member for three months, three for less than five years, one for ten years and one could not remember. There was a variation in the rate of consultation. One patient had visited her doctor several times, one 10 times and three 4 times or less and one could not remember. Three women had had their blood pressure checked in the last two years, two did not know and one said it had not been checked. Five women smoked and one did not. Of those who smoked, two said that the doctors had discussed smoking with them, two had not and one said it was not a discussion but a lecture and felt that doctors should not lecture, but find out why people smoked. Four respondents had relatives who suffered from either stroke (1), high blood pressure (1), diabetes and heart failure (1), and diabetes (1).

### d. White Women – Results of General Questionnaire

There were 18 white women screened but one of them was not registered with the Centre. Of the 17 women registered, three had been members for less than a year, two between 2–5 years; nine between 5–10 years; one since the Centre opened and one did not know. Consultations ranged from often – 3 patients; ten times – 2 patients; six times – 2 patients; three times – 1 patient; once – 1 patient; only when pregnant – 1 patient; don't know – 6 patients. Only one patient had not had her blood pressure measured in the past two years, and one could not remember. Ten women did not smoke and of the eight smokers three said doctors did discuss their smoking habits. Fourteen women had relatives suffering from cardio-vascular diseases and diabetes – high blood pressure 1, stroke 6, heart attack 1, diabetes 2, and four could not remember what condition in the above list relatives died of.

### e. Black Men – Results of the General Questionnaire

There were only two respondents in this category. One had been registered with the Centre for ten years and the other for one week. The first consulted over 20 times and the latter only once. Both had had their blood pressure checked in the last two years. One smoked and had discussed the problems posed by smoking with his doctors. The new member was not a smoker. Neither patient had relatives who had died or suffered from cardio-vascular diseases or diabetes.

### f. White Men – Results of the General Questionnaire

Fourteen patients responded to the questionnaire but one was not registered with the Centre.

**Table 8   Length of Time Registered with the Centre**

| | | |
|---|---|---|
| Over 10 years | — | 5 patients |
| Over 2 years | — | 5 patients |
| Under 1 year | — | 3 patients |

**Table 9   Number of Patients Who Visited Centre for Consultation in the Last Two Years**

| | |
|---|---|
| 1 | 35 times |
| 4 | 10 times |
| 5 | 7 times |
| 2 | 4 times |
| 1 | 3 times |

**Table 10   Blood Pressure Checks in the Last Two Years**

| | |
|---|---|
| 6 | In the last 2 years |
| 1 | 10 years ago |
| 1 | 5 years ago |
| 2 | 3 years ago |
| 4 | could not remember |

Of the fourteen patients, nine smoked. Seven had discussed their smoking habit with their doctors and since then two had stopped smoking. Thirteen had first degree relatives who had died or were suffering from cardio-vascular diseases or diabetes:

Stroke/high blood pressure/heart disease – 7
High blood pressure/diabetes          – 2
Can't remember which                  – 4

The question which asked patients to comment on the care they received from the Health Centre was, unfortunately, placed at the end of the section dealing with women's health. This may account for the small number of men who commented – four white men and one black man. Of the four, one did not think he wanted to make any comment, one felt it was 'ok', the other wanted to have more magazines and the fourth felt that the Centre was too slow, too long a time to wait after one had made an appointment. The black man thought the Centre 'does endeavour to get involved in the community it serves'.

Eight white and three black women commented on the Centre. Of the eight, five were very pleased with the Centre, one found it reasonable, one had not been there for long and felt she could not comment at that stage. The last patient had been seen by three different doctors for the same complaint. It was the third one who

**Table 11   Results of the Questionnaire on the Use of Well-Woman Clinics**
**White Women**

| Age | Knowledge about Well-woman Clinic | Have been to the Clinic | Would like to go to the Clinic | Knows how to make an Appointment | Had Cervical Smear | Prefer Male or Female |
|---|---|---|---|---|---|---|
| 62 | yes | no | no | no | yes | either |
| 45 | no | — | yes | no | yes | female |
| 37 | no | — | yes | no | yes | female |
| 30 | yes | no | no | no | yes | female |
| 69 | no | — | no | no | no | female |
| 37 | yes | yes | — | — | yes | either |
| 66 | yes | no | no | no | yes | either |
| 27 | think so | no | yes | no | yes | female |
| 27 | yes | no | no | yes | no | female |
| 22 | yes | no | yes | yes | no | either |
| 34 | yes | yes | — | — | yes | female |
| 38 | yes | yes | — | — | yes | female |
| 29 | vague | no | no | no | no | female |
| 38 | yes | yes | — | — | yes | female |
| 25 | no | — | yes | no | yes | either |
| 38 | yes | no | yes | no | no | either |
| 29 | yes | yes | — | — | yes | female |

**Table 12   Results of the Questionnaire on the Use of Well-Woman Clinics**
**Black Women**

| Age | Knowledge about Well-woman Clinic | Have been to the Clinic | Would like to go to the Clinic | Knows how to make an Appointment | Had Cervical Smear | Prefer Male or Female |
|---|---|---|---|---|---|---|
| 56 | yes | yes | — | — | yes | female |
| 38 | yes | yes | — | — | yes | female |
| 27 | yes | no | yes | yes | yes | female |
| 33 | yes | no | yes | no | yes | female |
| 23 | yes | no | no | no | yes | either |
| 25 | no | — | yes | no | yes | either |

took action and suggested tests. She was very unhappy about the first two doctors.

'The first two, by not listening, but making assumptions, could have prevented me from finding out if anything was wrong and doing anything about it.'

Of the three black women who commented two were generally pleased and the third felt that it was a

'Good Centre, good care. But more discussion needed over patients' smoking habits, more questions needed as to why patients smoke.'

## g. General Discussion

Given the small number of respondents it is not possible to draw meaningful conclusions from the results of the screening. There are, however, interesting and significant observations to be made from the results of the general questionnaire, despite the small size of the sample. It was encouraging to discover that 70% of the people screened had had their blood pressure measured in the last two years. Screening at regular intervals, as has been argued before, is the only effective way of detecting high blood pressure at its initial stage before irreparable damage is caused to the patient's health. The above results confirm that doctors in the Centre share this view. It was, however, depressing to note that despite all the measures aimed at discouraging people from smoking 57.5% in the sample were smokers, and only two of the fourteen who discussed this problem with their doctors had stopped the habit. What was more alarming was the high proportion of black women who smoked, 83% compared to white women 44%, white men 64% and black men 50%. Although the numbers of people in this sample are small these results are quite disturbing and they appear to support the comment made by a black woman respondent who suggested that what needs to be addressed is the reasons why people smoke. It was also interesting to note that more white men, 92%, had first degree relatives who died or suffered from cardio-vascular disease compared to white women 77% and black women 80%, and perhaps more significant that of the first degree relatives 60% were males and 40% females.

Of the 16 patients who commented on the health care received, 75% were generally pleased with the Centre, including the respondent who objected to the lectures on smoking. This response to smoking suggests that even in a Centre where patients are generally satisfied with the treatment, some of the doctors may still adopt an authoritarian attitude without knowing the full history. It is difficult to comment on the complaint of one patient who felt that the first two doctors who dealt with her condition made assumptions and, therefore, failed to carry out the necessary tests. It is possible that the third doctor had the benefit of the information compiled by the previous two and was therefore in a better position to decide that such tests were needed. On the other hand, it could be that the third doctor was more responsive to patients' anxiety and carried out tests in order to put their minds at rest. The significant aspect of this case, however, is that the patient felt free and safe to tell researchers about this incident in the knowledge that they were not part of the Centre and that the identity of the patients would never be revealed. It is clear from the results of the questionnaire that providers of health care, and this applies to all service providers, should from time to time evaluate the effectiveness of their services. The results of the evaluation, however, will only be meaningful if patients feel safe to be honest in answering the questions asked. It is possible that some of the 60% of people who made no comments did not feel safe to do so since the interviews were conducted at the Centre, even though the researchers were not part of the establishment.

The results on the Well-Woman clinic were quite interesting particularly as the Centre runs its own Well-Woman clinic. Of the 23 women (both black and white), 73% knew about the Well-Woman clinic and yet only 30% had visited it. 39% said they would like to go. 56% including those who did not want to visit the Well-Woman clinic said they would not know how to make an appointment. 78% of the sample had had a cervical smear. None of the women preferred a male doctor, 65% preferred a female doctor and 35% said either. It would be interesting to see the situation in Health Centres and Surgeries which do not provide the service of a Well-Woman clinic. But it is equally important for those who do provide such a service to realise that patients must be made aware of its availability. The high proportion of women preferring to be examined by a female doctor justifies the concern expressed to the Health Authority by the Health and Race Project researchers and the Community Health Council about the shortage of female doctors in the Health Service.

## 5. Hindu Centre

Prior to screening the researcher visited the Hindu Centre to talk in general about the Health and Race Project and in particular about screening. After consultation with a doctor who is a member of the community it was decided to offer urine testing, as members of the Asian community are believed to have a high incidence of diabetes. The researcher was advised to leave specimen bottles and forms with the caretaker and those interested in the screening would take bottles home and bring them with the specimen on Sunday at 3.00 p.m. when people normally arrive at the Centre for prayer. For four Sundays the researcher went to the Centre but only three people took up the service and none of them had sugar in their urine.

In discussing the non-uptake of the service with some members of the community two main reasons were given:

(a) The Hindu Centre has a Temple and when people come it is specifically for religious reasons and they would not want to mix their religious life with other activities, in particular not with urine testing.

(b) Not a lot of people came on these Sundays. The largest number was ten and we were told that many of them were related to doctors or were doctors themselves and therefore, would be having their health checks within their own family setting.

A doctor who is a member of the community stated that diabetes is quite common among Asians and in India there is now a Diabetic Society which is trying to come to grips with this condition. Although this screening was not successful it did provide the opportunity to inform members of the Centre about the Screening Project, asking them to let other members of the community know where the next screening was to take place should they want to be screened.

## 6. Somali Centre

In the past there has been very little contact between the Somali community as a whole and various statutory agencies in Liverpool including the Health Service. However, by 1985 this pattern was beginning to change. These changes are discussed in Consultative Paper Three below. The Health and Race Project had been particularly involved with Somali women and their health and in the course of that involvement a blood pressure screening session with women was arranged.

The women normally had their meetings on Sunday afternoon in a small room which served as an office for the Somali Community Worker in Cawdor Street in Liverpool 8. The room was not only small but was also very cold with a two-bar electric fire for heating. An attempt to find alternative accommodation for meetings had so far failed.

Twenty women attended the screening session; 19 of them were African and only one was a British born black woman. Their ages ranged between 25 and 54 years. One woman aged 47 had a blood pressure of 150/100. None of the remaining participants had diastolic pressure above 95 mm Hg or systolic pressure above 140 mm Hg. The screening on this session was carried out by the researcher from the Health and Race Project with the assistance of a health visitor who worked in the area.

The screening was one reason for the meeting. The other was to meet and ask questions of a general practitioner who had been invited by the women, and also to ask the health visitor questions on child health and development. This was a successful session and the areas covered included AIDS, cervical cancer, breast cancer, diabetes, vertigo, cervical smears, contraception, menstruation and consti-pation. The discussions were conducted through an interpreter. The health visitor explained her role in the community.

Women gained so much in that meeting that a decision was made to continue these health classes at times agreed to suit all participants. The women were to draw up a list of areas to be discussed and the doctor, health visitor and Health and Race Project researcher would attend the sessions together or separately depending on their other commitments.

One area of concern was the lack of information of various health topics. This was particularly expressed in the area of AIDS where there are no leaflets available in Somali or Arabic. Enquiries were made in Liverpool about the possibility of having such leaflets trans-lated into appropriate languages since these were not available from elsewhere.

One area that created a lot of debate in the group was the suggest-ion by the media during that week that AIDS started in Africa. This suggestion followed a statement made about an AIDS virus being isolated in Africa 20 years ago. Women argued that if that was the case there must be evidence of African villages which were decimated by the AIDS virus in the last 20 years, and there is no such evidence. There were strong feelings about the racist and political implications of the media suggestions.

## 7. Pakistan Centre

At the time of this research project the Pakistan Centre had a Manpower Services Commission temporary employment scheme with approximately 15 workers, some of whom were interested in health issues. The scheme ran a magazine with material written in three languages, English, Urdu and Arabic. After approaching the Manager of the Project the researchers were asked to write a short article on the Health and Race Project for the magazine which had a wide readership, including people who lived in Scotland. In the article people were invited to come for screening, and details of the arrangements were also given. In addition letters were written which the MSC workers sent to families on their lists, informing them that screening was to be held in the Centre on the 3rd March 1987 between 9.30 a.m. and 1.00 p.m.

Twelve people were screened – eight females and four males. One woman was from India, six were from Pakistan and one was a British white woman. All four men were from Pakistan. Table 13 shows the result of screening:

**Table 13  Pakistan Centre Screening Result**

| Nationality | Age | Male | Female | B.P. | Urine | Comments |
|---|---|---|---|---|---|---|
| Pakistani | 29 | 1 | | 110/80 | n/d | |
| Pakistani | 53 | 1 | | 130/80 | neg. | On treatment for diabetes |
| Pakistani | — | 1 | | 120/70 | n/d | |
| Pakistani | 20 | 1 | | 100/78 | n/d | |
| Indian | 40 | | 1 | 140/90 | 1% | Fasting specimen Not known as diabetic |
| Pakistani | 40 | | 1 | 130/90 | neg. | |
| Pakistani | 25 | | 1 | 110/70 | neg. | |
| Pakistani | 35 | | 1 | 110/70 | n/d | |
| Pakistani | 26 | | 1 | 90/70 | n/d | |
| Pakistani | — | | 1 | 120/80 | neg. | |
| Pakistani | 27 | | 1 | 100/80 | n/d | |
| British W | 37 | | 1 | 108/70 | n/d | |
| TOTAL | | 4 | 8 | | | |

n/d = not done     neg. = negative

## a. Results of Screening

Out of 12 people only six people wanted their urine tested. One of them had 1% sugar in her urine and neither herself nor her doctor was aware of this problem. One man had no sugar in his urine but he was on treatment for diabetes and he started having diabetes in 1975. He was also on treatment for angina. One woman whose urine was negative had had a blood sugar test when in Pakistan and it was positive. She was at the time awaiting arrangements to have a blood sugar test with her doctor. One woman who had a negative urine test had a mother who had diabetes and both the parents of one man suffered from high blood pressure.

Again very small numbers are being dealt with here but it is interesting, in the light of the existing literature which suggests that people of Asian origin tend to suffer more from diabetes, that out of six people whose urine was tested three had diabetic problems: one on treatment, one newly detected and one to have further tests to confirm the condition.

The results of screening were, as usual, sent to the individual doctors and the woman who had 1% sugar in her urine was advised to go and see her doctor, which she did. The doctor tested her urine and it was positive. The doctor referred the patient to hospital where hopefully she would be put on treatment for diabetes.

Helping with the screening was a Pakistani MSC worker and this was not only useful in terms of easing the workload but also in serving as interpreter as most of the women spoke very little English. It also created a very relaxed and friendly atmosphere because both researcher and MSC worker had met some of the women previously during the home visits. What was more important was that the MSC worker was from the community and had known all the women socially and had been involved in their health problems. That relationship is crucial in the area of take-up of services.

There was also present in the screening session a health visitor who had clients in this community. This again was very helpful as some people discussed child care issues. One woman had brought her child's urine. The child had been to hospital for investigation because he was passing 'white' urine. The explanation given to the parents was that there were white cells in the urine. The child still on occasions passes 'white' urine but the doctor had said not to worry about it. The parents are still very worried because they did not understand what was happening. The health visitor in the screening session intended to follow this up with the doctor and to try to get more information for the parents.

During the screening session there was a brief visit from the dietician who arranged to come to the Centre when she could see people who were interested in dieting in general or those who wanted to discuss a diabetic diet. It was hoped that this would lead to the establishment of a Diabetic Clinic in the Pakistan Centre.

Although only 12 people were screened in this session we were encouraged by the response and more sessions were arranged at intervals and with a wider publicity in order to encourage more people to come forward for screening.

## 8. Merseyside Community Relations Council

Although respondents here did not belong to any one particular centre or surgery, they were still asked to fill in the questionnaire. Nine people were screened – six women and three men. The age range varied between 24 and 38 years. All but one did not have high blood pressure. All of them had been with their respective doctors for no less than three years. The longest was 26 years. Consultations varied between one and six times in the last two years. Eight had had their blood pressure checked and one could not remember. Six people smoked and three had discussed this problem with their doctors. Five had relatives who suffered from one of the diseases mentioned above.

*The evaluation of services received from Centre/Surgery*

Not all respondents commented on the quality of care they received from their doctors. The three comments were:

1. 'Not enough information about problems relating to black people's health.'
2. 'I think doctors should not operate sophisticated reception services, simply because of confidentiality. I also think women doctors should be available on request and family planning services ought to be available every day at the doctor's surgery not just at certain times.'
3. 'Convenient health service for women i.e. family planning and Well-Woman Clinic.'

## 9. General Conclusions on Screening

The number of people screened in both Health and Community

Centres does not allow any firm conclusions to be made about the propensity of black people to suffer more from high blood pressure and diabetes than white people. However, in the course of screening a number of important observations relevant to primary health care were made.

Firstly it is crucial that screening becomes an integral part of health care. This is particularly important for high blood pressure and diabetes where a patient only becomes aware of the illness after some damage has been done to the body. Early detection of these conditions through regular screening can avoid prolonged medications and their inherent damaging side effects. It is also cost effective since an early detection may, in some cases, mean that some form of treatment other than medication and hospitalization can be recommended.

Secondly, the number of people who were eager to find out more about health issues, including the process of taking blood pressure, exploded the myth that people are not interested in their own health. Most people felt that more information should be available, not necessarily from their doctors since they were busy during surgery hours but from someone who had time to talk and to answer questions on health issues and procedures in general, in a way that is easily understood. In other words, the people in this study were asking for a demystification of health care.

Thirdly it is important for primary health care workers to be aware of the limitations of screening only those people who are 'patients'. This is not health care but 'disease care'. There is a need to establish screening in the community before people become patients with the above conditions. Health care must go to the people. This will involve the development of a network of neighbourhood health workers who should be an integral part of the primary health team.

Fourthly, it was clear that it was not enough to provide a service if it is not sufficiently well advertised to patients. Written notices in a Health Centre/Surgery are not the most effective way of attracting a patient's attention. Talking to people, or the use of videos whilst patients are waiting to be seen, are two of the ways in which information can be effectively imparted to patients. This, of course, must take into account the use of interpreters where there are patients whose mother tongue is not English.

Finally, it seems crucial that providers of health care must have some means of evaluating the effectiveness of their services. This is no more than 'good practice'. If it is not known whether or not what is provided is good quality, then it is not possible to improve the service. The evaluation must not be merely disease oriented. It must be holistic, promoting health rather than just curing disease. Health Centres must be Health Centres in reality, otherwise they might as well be called 'Disease Centres'.

# The Somali Community – Their Health Needs

The approach to health issues in this research is comprehensive in that it has as its starting point the World Health Organisation's definition which sees health as:

> 'A state of complete physical, mental and social well-being and not merely the absence of disease or infirmity.'[1]

In this context, health is not primarily seen in terms of the malfunctioning of a mechanical system within which, as Doyal points out, treatment is usually seen to consist of chemical, surgical or even electrical intervention to restore the normal functioning of the machine.[2] This is a very narrow definition which obscures the links between ill-health and the social, political and economic factors. Such factors are crucial in determining the degree of health enjoyed by the individual. It is for this reason that when the health needs of the Somali community are considered, their total experience, as perceived by them, in the environment in which they find themselves will be taken into account.

Although the Somali community was one of the first racial minority groups to settle in Liverpool, few people know anything about or have had contact with this community. The researchers' own involvement intensified from the beginning of the present Project. At the end of 1986 the secretary to the Merseyside Somali Community Association produced a report on the survey he had carried out on the Somali community in Liverpool.[3] This report has not only helped to highlight some of the problems faced by this community but has also given background information on the Somalis in Liverpool and this paper draws heavily on the contents of that report.

## 1. The Somali Population in Liverpool

Many Somali people came to Britain during the First World War. They were mainly seamen and therefore tended to settle in British ports including Liverpool. But the majority of the Somali people came to Britain in the 1950's to meet the shortage of labour on British ships. In recent years more Somali people have come to Britain as refugees from the political situation in their own country.

According to the report there are 233 known Somali households in Liverpool and out of these 186 have been surveyed:

### Table 14   Surveyed Households

| Ages | 0–7 | 8–11 | 12–16 | 17–25 | 26–45 | 45–65 | 65–75 | 75+ |
|---|---|---|---|---|---|---|---|---|
| 120 Single Households | | | 1 | 6 | 16 | 72 | 23 | 2 |
| 66 Families | 60 | 29 | 52 | 48 | 49 | 55 | 7 | — |
| TOTALS | 60 | 29 | 53 | 54 | 65 | 127 | 30 | 2 |
| Female | 38 | 11 | 17 | 10 | 27 | 31 | 1 | — |
| Male | 22 | 18 | 36 | 44 | 38 | 96 | 29 | 2 |
| TOTALS | 60 | 29 | 53 | 54 | 65 | 127 | 30 | 2 |

(Merseyside Somali Community Association/CSV Project).

Most of the Somalis live in Liverpool 8 in the Toxteth area. Of those surveyed 173 reside in this area and only 13 are scattered in other parts of the city.

### Table 15   Somalis Living Outside Toxteth

| | |
|---|---|
| Norris Green | 2 |
| Aigburth | 2 |
| Mossley Hill | 2 |
| Wavertree | 4 |
| Rainhill | 1 |
| City Centre | 1 |
| Dingle | 1 |
| TOTAL | 13 |

There were a total of 42ᴜ members in the 186 Somali households surveyed.

Although the Somali community, like most inner city dwellers, face problems of deprivation, the general feeling of members of this community is that they suffer more than any other group in areas of employment, housing, health, education and social facilities. 42% of Somalis are from Commonwealth countries i.e. Kenya, Uganda and Tanzania. It is this particular group, the report states, which feels worse off, and not treated like other Commonwealth citizens. The situation has been exacerbated by a sense of isolation and, until recently, a lack of communication with either statutory or voluntary organisations. This has meant that the community has not been able to articulate its needs strongly and consistently.

Prior to 1985 the Somali community had a Centre with a full-time Development Worker. The Centre served as a source of information and place where the community met and discussed their situation. This Centre was closed in 1985 because the building was unsafe. At the moment they have no Centre and only a part-time Development Worker who operates from a small upstairs office.

## 2. Employment

The level of unemployment within the Somali community is very high. Out of 186 households surveyed only a few heads of households were employed. The rest, as Table 16 shows, are unemployed, in full-time education or retired.

**Table 16   Occupation of Surveyed Somalis**

| | |
|---|---|
| Employed | 7 |
| Unemployed | 230 |
| Housewives | 32 |
| Full-time Education | 71 |
| Children 7 years and under | 50 |
| Retired | 30 |
| TOTAL | 420 |

(Merseyside Somali Community Association/CSV Project)

Most Somalis came to Britain to work on ships, and the decline in this sector of industry has left many without jobs. But even with the younger generation the problem of unemployment still exists. Only two young people were on Youth Training Schemes at the time of the survey.

Of the seven employed people one was on low income. That means that only six of the 420 people surveyed had a reasonable standard of living and that invariably has implications for the health of the community.

## 3. Housing

The situation in housing is no better. Since most people are on social security it is not possible to have extra money for repairs. Owner-occupied homes are on the whole damp and in need of major repairs. Those who are tenants of Housing Associations, Local Authority or privately rented property vary in the degree of satisfaction with their housing accommodation. Some, according to the report, are dissatisfied and would like to move. It is interesting to note that the lowest number of tenants – a total of eight – is with the Local Authority as opposed to 68 in privately rented accommodation, 26 owner-occupiers and 60 with Housing Associations. This supports the findings of a Housing Report which revealed that good Local Authority housing is not easily available to racial minorities in Liverpool.[4]

## 4. Education

It was not until 1972 that Somali became a written language. Prior to that period 90% of the population in Somalia could neither read nor write. The remaining 10% were literate in some or all of the following languages: English, French, Italian and Arabic. Among those who are over the age of 18 years in Liverpool there is still a very high level of illiteracy. In the survey less than 20 people could read and write fluently. The majority could neither read nor write whilst a few could just about read and write. Among the younger generation English is the main language used in their education in Britain but the Somali community feel that:

> 'The children who are born here should also be taught to read and write their own language to prepare them to settle in Somalia if they ever decided to go and live there.'[5]

But apart from preparing for this eventuality, language is an important part of identification and the development of a positive self-image for any group.

The adult members of the community also feel that they need to learn English in order to communicate with the providers in the host country.

## 5. The Elders

Of the 420 people who took part in the survey 32, all males, were over the age of 65. 127 (31 women and 96 men) were between 45 and 65 years old. This is a clear indication that the needs of this group are going to increase. Most of the elderly are single men living on their own. They are isolated and have no common place to meet and discuss the problems they face. Two schemes have been initiated to try and meet some of these problems.

### a. Supported Group Homes

This was an initiative of Liverpool Personal Services Society in conjunction with Merseyside Improved Houses, representatives from Social Services (Senior Adviser for the Elderly) and the Somali community. A small terraced house has been modernised and fully furnished with a part-time carer to cater for three elderly Somali men who are now tenants. The running costs of the house i.e. electricity, gas, telephone, carer's wages, etc are met under the Board and Lodging Section and Hostel Accommodation Allowances from the DHSS.[6] The cost of the house conversion was £35,000.

The house was opened in 1985. It is a three bedroomed house with a communal lounge where the men can socialise and also have friends visiting them. There is a separate room which is used as a prayer room. This is a good start but more such homes are needed urgently to meet the number of those in need of this form of accommodation. Liverpool Personal Services Society are still involved in the scheme and more homes, not just for the Somali community but for other groups as well, are in the pipeline. By March 1987 they had opened a four bedroomed house for elderly people from the Caribbean community. At that time there were only two tenants with a third one in the process of negotiating the prospect of joining the group.

### b. Meals on Wheels

The majority of the Somali people are Muslims. When the Meals on Wheels for the Muslim community was set up by Social Services some of the Somali elders were included as recipients of this service. However, the Somali community reported that this arrangement was not satisfactory because the service did not provide Somali meals and in consequence the elders from this community did not eat the meals. Some Somali elders only received milk delivered from this service and this created concern and demonstrated a need to look at more appropriate ways of providing this service. There were 41 elderly men, 39 of whom were single, who would benefit if a more acceptable service was available.

## 6. Women

Within the community women were faced with multiple problems. Most of the women came to join their husbands who worked as seamen. Most of the time they are in the home with children since in the inner city there are no facilities for children to play. In addition most women cannot speak English and this creates difficulties in terms of shopping, travelling and the use of social, health and school services. For most of their lives the Somali women feel isolated from the host society as well as from each other as there is no Centre where they and their children can meet to socialise. In the first meeting attended by the researchers this feeling of being 'boxed-in' was seen as responsible for causing depression for some members of the group.

## 7. Social and Leisure Facilities

Before 1985 the Somali community had the use of a house which they used as a Centre. There was a full-time Community Worker who advised people on various issues or directed them to relevant organisations. The Centre was also used for social meetings as well as classes for those who wanted to learn English as a second language. In 1985 this house was closed down because, it was stated, the building was structurally unsafe.

Since then the community has had no Centre. They have had the use of a room in a small terraced house in Cawdor Street. The house belongs to Merseyside Improved Houses in conjunction with Liverpool Personal Services Society and was earmarked as a property for another group home for the Somali elders. The room was mainly for the use of a part-time Development Worker but was often used for meetings. The size of the room is approximately 12' × 12'. In winter it is bitterly cold as there is no central heating. The only source of heating is a two-bar movable electric heater. In one meeting on a Sunday afternoon there were 25 women some of whom had brought children with them. Not only was lack of space the problem, there was also anxiety about the safety of the children with regards to the precarious form of heating as well as the danger of falling down the steep stairs which they were using as play space.

At the time of this research, the house in Cawdor Street was to be closed down as work to convert it to a group home was to begin. The community was offered the use of the Pakistan Centre, but this poses financial problems as they would have to pay £15.00 to use the Centre for two hours. This is a lot of money to find in a community where most of the members are unemployed. A Community Centre for the Somalis is crucial. Most of the new initiatives are dependent on the quick availability of a Centre for their full realisation and progression.

## 8. New Initiatives

There were a number of new initiatives that took place within the Somali community in an attempt to meet the desperate needs outlined above. Some of these were linked to two organisations that took a particular interest in the community following the initial approach to them by members of the Somali community. One was the Business In The Community and the other was the Community Service Volunteers (CSV). The former is concerned with creating economic life within the community and focusses on job skills training which will eventually lead to job creation. The second has interests in community development programmes related to social welfare. Both organisations are London-based but representatives attended regular meetings with the Somali community in Liverpool. There was a Steering Committee with representatives from Social Services, education, housing and the Health and Race Project.

Although the main focus of this study is on health an input was made into other areas which as stated earlier are crucial in determining the health status of a community. Below is a brief account of some progress that was made in these new initiatives.

## 9. Education

The College that has had a large input in this area is Millbrook. Some lecturers in this College were invited to a meeting to discuss the possibility of setting up classes for the Somali community. Until then some Somalis had been attending English as a second language in Windsor Street where most of the teachers were white and did not speak Somali or Arabic. The suggestion at the meeting was that classes be established in the community in both English and Somali and they should, where possible, be taught by Somalis. Although there were Somalis who spoke English and Somali, such individuals did not have teaching skills. Millbrook College put on a course to teach such skills. The course was to run for 13–14 weeks. Two Somalis attended the course, one woman who was to teach female students and one man for male students.

In the meantime classes were established in Cawdor Street. A small room was used as a classroom. There were two female teachers: one taught English for two days (two hours each day) and the other taught Somali for two days (two hours each day). There were also two male teachers; one taught English and one taught Somali. The English teachers were still students in Millbrook College and their teaching, for which they received payment, was supervised and assessed by a tutor from Millbrook. One of the teachers (student) subsequently left the country. Her teaching post was to be covered by a teacher from Millbrook. The Somali teaching was done by people who spoke very little English and they would be taught teaching skills by those at present at the College, once they qualified.

The attendance in both sets of classes was good and both groups had about 15 people on the register. The main drawback was lack of space and facilities. This educational work should be extended to include children who, the community felt, should have the opportunity to learn Somali as well as receive religious instruction. But without a Centre with appropriate facilities this could not be done. There are many other courses that the Somalis would like to have. A course in welfare rights, for example, is crucial in a community that depends for its livelihood on social security. There are discussions about the possibility of other courses, e.g. book-keeping, typing, computers etc, that may increase skills in the community and hopefully lead to employment.

## 10. The Elders

The plight faced by the elderly who are mainly single men living on their own has already been discussed. Only three have appropriate accommodation in a supported group home and another house for another three to four people is soon to be converted by Liverpool Personal Services Society in conjunction with Merseyside Improved Houses. But this will not be sufficient for the 41 + elderly who need accommodation. The Health and Race Project had initial discussions with the Chairman of Abbeyfield, an organisation which provides accommodation for the elderly, but this area has now been passed on to the Chairman of Bilal Housing Association. At a meeting on May

5th 1987 the Bilal Chairman reported that discussions with Abbeyfield had been held in abeyance in view of the offer from Merseyside Improved Houses to provide a training course in housing for the black community. Merseyside Improved Houses had already submitted an application for a £100,000 grant to the Housing Corporation to assist black housing organisations. Bilal has already been granted £38,000 by the Housing Corporation through Merseyside Improved Houses and this funding will be used to renovate a house which might be used for the elderly.

The lack of take-up of Meals on Wheels has been investigated by the social services Senior Adviser for the Elderly. The possibility of having a Somali cook in order to provide acceptable meals within the existing Muslim Meals on Wheels scheme was to be explored.

Age Concern was also invited to a meeting in which the needs of the elderly were discussed. The representative from this organisation hinted that they would be prepared to provide free meals if the Somalis had a Day Centre where such meals could be provided. Age Concern would also be willing to contribute £1,000 towards the purchase of a property which would serve as a Day Centre. Such a property would cost approximately £7,000. But, of course, if the Somalis had a Community Centre the problem of premises for a Day Centre would not arise.

## 11. Health

This is the area in which the Health and Race Project is directly involved, and so far the focus has been, for obvious reasons, mainly on women. At the first meeting which was attended by 20 women a number of problem areas were identified:

### a. Language Difficulties

This, as stated earlier, creates problems on a day-to-day basis when women want to go shopping, travelling or communicating with teachers at their children's school. But it becomes desperate when women have to visit a doctor for themselves or their children. The women who were at the meeting had never been offered an interpreter in a hospital. Some of them stated that they had to wait for days before they could have someone from the community (a friend, and in some cases to wait for a husband to come back from sea) to accompany them and interpret during a consultation with a General Practitioner. But even the interpreter may not be fluent in English and definitely not familiar with medical terms that health professionals use. When no interpreter is available, one receptionist said that hand language is used:

'This is quite satisfactory. We understand each other well.'

But the Somali women did not think that this was satisfactory. Most of the time they did not know what the doctor or receptionist was saying and they could not explain to them what their medical problems were. The whole experience is a source of anxiety for most women.

### b. The Need for Female Doctors

For religious and cultural reasons Somali women do not want to be examined by a male doctor. This is particularly the case in areas of ante-natal/post-natal and gynaecological examinations. The situation is worse in hospitals where sometimes they are faced with a crowd of medical students and there is no one to explain what is going on. For these reasons many women are reluctant to use hospital services.

One of the requests the women made was to have a session with a General Practitioner in which they could ask her all the questions they have never been able to discuss with their own G.P.s. A local G.P. agreed to come to a meeting together with a health visitor. A number of topics were discussed superficially and screening for high blood pressure was carried out. The women expressed a desire for the continuation of the sessions and they said they would draw up a list of topics to be examined in depth. The G.P., health visitor and the researcher were to take part in the discussion. But the problem in finding suitable premises made this difficult.

The discussions were conducted through an interpreter. This is not a very satisfactory form of health education particularly as women want to get involved in Women and Health courses. A more satisfactory way of providing this form of health education is through the Somali language which all women understand. Part of the way forward therefore would be to set up a Women and Health course for Somali tutors and provide them with a training pack and background support. When they have enough knowledge and confidence they can then communicate that information to other women in Somali. This is the best way, particularly for pregnant women who need to know very quickly what to expect when they go to ante-natal clinics and when in hospital for childbirth. The problem was that the few women who were bilingual were still undertaking the course at Millbrook College and they still needed to find their feet teaching English before more work could be put on them. But even when women and health classes are given by trained Somali women there will still be a need for the women to continue the sessions with the health professionals because this achieves more than just an exchange of information. It breaks the barriers and enables women to meet health professionals on their own territory as it were. The atmosphere is relaxed and women know they can ask questions without feeling threatened.

## 12. The Somali Women's Group

Most of the women who were involved in the health group were also members of the Somali Women's Group. The Chairperson who initiated the Group did so because 'in the Muslim society a woman cannot socialise' and she seldom ventures out of her family setting. This creates problems particularly as the children remain also isolated from different play-schemes available to their counterparts in the city. The Group was anxious to develop a summer play-scheme for the children. Unfortunately, they had no funds and they had difficulty in getting money from charities because they had no charitable status at the time. But the Group made contact with many voluntary organisations all of which were willing to give them help and support. The Group consisted of 37 women and 115 children and in an attempt to raise funds the women paid a subscription fee of £2.00 a month.

Apart from the work with children the coming together as a group generated a lot of confidence among women which enabled them to venture beyond the boundaries of Merseyside. On the 28th March 1987 12 of the women and 14 children went by coach to attend a one-day conference organised by the Foundation for Women's Development and Research. The conference was organised to discuss the question of female circumcision and was an interesting and exciting development and might hopefully link Liverpool Somali women with other Somali women in other parts of the country and, with the advance in language ability, link Somali women with all other women facing racism, classism and sexism.

Real progress in the initiatives started by the Somali community is very much dependent on the immediate availability of suitable premises for a Community Centre. Here can be established courses in various fields, a Day Centre for the elderly, distribution of Meals on Wheels, nursery group and leisure activities as well as the advisory service in welfare rights. It is therefore crucial that both statutory and voluntary sectors work together to establish such a Centre as soon as possible.

# References

1. World Health Organisation.

2. Doyal, L., *The Political Economy of Health*, Pluto, 1980.

3. Yusuf, E. M., *The Somali Population in Liverpool*, Merseyside Somali Community Association/CSV Project, 1986 (unpublished).

4. Law, I. *et al*, *Race and Housing in Liverpool*, Commission for Racial Equality, 1984.

5. Yusuf, E. M., *op cit*, p. 6.

6. Finn, J. and Abendstern, J., *Supported Group Living for Ethnic Elders*, Liverpool Personal Services Society, 1986.

# Black and Ethnic Minority Elders

In the area of elderly people one of the recent and perhaps the most outstanding studies is the one conducted by Bhalla *et al* in Birmingham. The research outlines the poor health care received by elderly people. A sizeable proportion of the 'elders', the researchers stated, were receiving no treatment for eyes, feet, ears or teeth 'despite the fact that over two-thirds had seen their GP within the last month'.[1] Many remained isolated, unaware of facilities provided by Social Services and they were not visited by a Social Worker.

There is no similar study of the Health Service in Liverpool. A review of Social Services in the city has shown that the most 'scandalous' shortfall in services was in relation to the elders from black and ethnic minorities. A survey undertaken by the Specialist and Black Immigrant Social Workers Project Team in 1976 revealed the paucity of black and Chinese elders who were receiving Home Help Service, Day Care and Residential Care.[2] In 1978, a further survey by Fru confirmed the findings of the Project Team by showing that out of a total of 1,300 elderly people in sheltered accommodation only two were from racial minorities. The Home Help Service was provided for 1,106 white people while only ten racial minority elders received this service. Only seven racial minority elders received Day Care as opposed to 563 white elderly people. Meals on Wheels was received by 2,991 persons of whom only nine were black.[3]

The tendency for the providers when confronted with such hard evidence has been to explain the situation in terms of lack of knowledge by racial minorities about what is available, or by saying that black people do not use the service because they have strong kinship support or that there are no black elders because most black people prefer and do go back to their countries of origin when they reach old age. Contrary to these explanations the Specialist and Black Immigrant Social Workers Project Team always maintained that the problem was that of institutionalised racism:

> 'These figures give what is and will be recognised as some of the most substantial evidence available in Britain of "institutionalised" racism in action.'[4]

The Team argued that the shortfall in service was total and felt that

'it would be self-deluding and dishonest to try to explain it in a way that ignores not only a local, but national perspective of racial discrimination. We must therefore conclude that the failure to provide service for the black elderly of the city is a direct manifestation and result of institutionalised racism.'[5]

Credence to the Team's assertion was provided in the form of the results achieved by a Social Worker whose job was to locate black elders in the community. This case study of a 'Detached Social Worker for Black Elders' presented by Rooney in his recent work *Racism and Resistance to Change* explodes the myth about the absence of black elders in Liverpool. The work was carried out for two years and when it was terminated in 1985 the social worker had in her case load 52 black elderly people. The study therefore categorically established that:

'there were Black elders, that they resided in the districts which covered the Liverpool 8 area, that they had need of and wanted a range of the supportive services provided through those districts and that, by and large, they were not getting them in the normal course of events.'[6]

In discussing in detail the situation of black elderly people within Social Services in Liverpool the aim is not to digress from the field of health which is the main concern. On the contrary, examples from Social Services are used to draw parallels with what is happening to the black elderly people in the Health Service.

At the beginning of the Health and Race Project consultations and discussions were held with a variety of people. Amongst those consulted were nurses, doctors, health social workers, home helps as well as people in contact with the elderly people in the community e.g. relatives and neighbours. From the community there have been suggestions indicating that black elderly people were not gaining access to secondary care. But unlike the situation in Social Services there is no data in the Health Service to indicate the extent of the problem in terms of numbers of racial minority elderly people using the hospital service.

Whilst most health workers agreed that they did not see a lot of the racial minority elderly people in hospitals, the reasons given for their absence varied. Some gave similar kinds of explanations which had been encountered in Social Services: 'There are no black elderly

D

people here.' 'When they get old they prefer to return to their countries of origin.' 'They are looked after by their relatives because they have a strong kinship system.' 'They don't suffer from the diseases of the affluent.' 'They don't know about what is available so we must push health promotion.' A few suggested that institutionalised racism might be the reason.

In Nottingham, in 1987, Ebrahim *et al* carried out a study on the Asian, Caribbean and British born black elderly people. The researchers were

'concerned that elderly immigrants might be less likely to be admitted to hospital than indigenous people.'[7]

To test this hypothesis discharge dates from Hospital Activity Analysis were examined. The population estimated to be at risk living in the area under study comprised 219 Asian, 310 Caribbean and 88,717 white British born. The study covered the period between 1979–1983. Although in this study researchers found differences in terms of illness affecting different racial groups their original hypothesis was not proven:

'Although we had started our investigation with a suspicion that elderly immigrants were under-using hospital resources for a variety of reasons, ranging from insensitivity of the service to under-reporting of health problems, we found no evidence to support this contention.'[8]

Despite the results of the Nottingham study there remained concern about the responses from health workers and community members about the use of hospital services by elderly people from racial minorities in Liverpool. In order to pursue this, medical social workers on geriatric wards were approached to monitor the number of black and racial minority elderly people with whom they came into contact in three of these wards. At the time the medical social workers were approached the then existing City Council was against monitoring but the Director of Social Services through the Department's Research Officer suggested that medical social workers could give their 'impressions' of the situation.

Although this was not a satisfactory way of estimating the number of black and racial minority elders using the service a form was devised with the medical social workers which was to help them in the construction of their 'impressions'. The period covered in collecting this information was between August 1st 1986 to August 30th

1987. The number of black and racial minority elders who were admitted in these three wards, according to the forms from social workers is as follows:

**Table 17**

| Nationality | Sex | Age | Date of Admission |
|---|---|---|---|
| African | Male | 92 | 13th October 1986 |
| Chinese (Hong Kong) | Female | 78 | 13th October 1986 |
| British Black | Female | 83 | 18th May 1987 |
| African | Male | 73 | 3rd October 1986 |
| African (Yemen) | Male | 88 | 18th May 1987 |
| South Asian | Female | 80 | — |
| African | Male | 80 | — |
| Chinese | Female | 80 | — |
| Total | 8 | | |

Of the above eight, six were new admissions since 1st August 1986 whereas two were re-admissions since that date. Three were discharged home with services, two did not require services on discharge, one was admitted to residential care, one remained in long-term hospital care with a view to placement in residential care and one was discharged to the family's care. Of the eight patients three required an interpreter: an African male patient, 80 years old; a Chinese female patient, 78 years old and a Chinese female patient, 80 years old.

The results of this pilot study are very interesting but they cannot be used as a strong basis from which to draw conclusions about the number of elderly people. It is very possible that, with the heavy load that medical social workers have, some black and racial minority elderly people were not entered on the forms. In addition, elderly patients admitted from residential homes are not allocated to medical social workers. The senior medical social worker acts as a liaison officer between the home and the ward, and in some cases this is done by phone so that the medical social worker would not necessarily know whether the patient was a member of a racial minority. But notwithstanding all this, these figures remain interesting when it is considered that they come from three wards, each with an approximately 24 bed capacity (one of which had a total of 560 admissions between August 1986 and August 1987) and that the estimated number of black and ethnic minority people over the age of 60 years in Liverpool is between 2,250 and 4,500.

As a result of this pilot study, there are grounds for concern about the health of, and the services available to, the black elderly and therefore it is important that more work is done in this area to find out at what stage are problems encountered in the use of hospital services. To this end an application has been put forward to the Ethical Committee with a view to enabling researchers to conduct a more systematic monitoring of the hospital services with regards to their use by racial minorities. This application was put forward in December 1986 and three months later the researchers were informed that it was passed on to the Unit General Manager in the Royal Liverpool Hospital as it was deemed not to be medical research. To date no response has been received from the Unit General Manager.

A systematic research in this area is vital because if, in fact, there is an under-use of beds by elderly people from racial minorities it is important to find out why this is happening. It will be necessary to know who refers the patients to hospital and for what conditions. This then will move the focus away from hospitals to primary health care.

## References

1. Bhalla, A. and Blakemore, K., *Elders of the Minority Ethnic Group*, AFFOR, Birmingham, 1981.

2. Specialist Immigrant and Black Social Workers Project, 'Residential Care for the Elderly', Community Hostels, 1976, *Working Paper*.

3. Fru, F., *Survey of Black Elderly in Liverpool*, 1978.

4. Working Party on the Black Elderly, Paper No. 1.

5. Ibid.

6. Rooney, B., *Racism and Resistance to Change*, Merseyside Area Profile Group, Sociology Department, University of Liverpool, 1987, p. 66.

7. Ebrahim Shah *et al*, 'Elderly Immigrants – A Disadvantaged Group?', *Age and Ageing 1987*, 16, 249–255.

8. Ibid.

# The Interpreting Service

'Whilst on holiday abroad in May 1987 our 6 year old son slipped on a wet marble floor. For a few seconds he appeared to lie still and then seemed to shudder. We were terrified and bewildered as he wouldn't stop crying to answer any questions we asked about how he felt. The local residents rang for an ambulance which took us to the nearest hospital. Here the casualty doctor luckily spoke English. However, in view of our son's lack of memory about the incident and the possible convulsion this doctor suggested that I should go with our son to another hospital 40 miles away for X-rays and expert assessment.

I remember sitting with the ambulance man and two other patients – no one spoke English. Our son was crying and was violently sick all over me and himself and we sat there wet and smelling. There were no reassuring voices but only the driver who kindly drove faster to get us there.

On entering casualty in this hospital no one spoke English, no recognisable uniforms. I didn't know who was a doctor, a nurse, an orderly or cleaner. Again no reassuring voices from other patients; smiles and nods but no one to say not to worry he would be alright. I hung on to our son, my passport and my money in that order. We transferred between casualty, X-ray and the neurologist again under the wing of the ambulance man who used gestures to tell me to come, stop or wait.

The neurologist fortunately spoke English and she recommended admission for observation in case our son had had a convulsion. I spluttered incoherently, feeling my appearance and ignorance at just speaking one language made me look more of an idiot. Eventually we compromised on hourly supervision throughout the night by me, back in the hotel, and a further appointment, later in the week. Strenuous efforts were made to explain that I could not starve my son for the next 24 hours due to a congenital condition. I was nearly in tears by then wanting the support of my husband, home, my own General Practitioner – anyone who would comfort, console and interpret what I was trying to say. Eventually, another compromise –

24 hours on coke only, and a return to hospital immediately if I noticed any change or I could not wake him.

Bouncing back over the 40 miles I felt sick, my son slept, oblivious to the smell of vomit still all over us. I had with me his X-rays and a report from casualty which meant absolutely nothing to me. On arrival at the hotel – 6 hours later – my husband was more than relieved to see us, having had no idea where we were or whether our son had fractured his skull or not. The interpreter read the report from casualty for us. It read 'baby kicked in head, mother refused admission'. I cried then, feeling sorry for us, my ability to communicate without knowledge of the language had obviously been a dismal failure.

Looking back, I realised how dependent I am for reassurance by knowing the system of the health service, which door to enter, where to stand, where to find a toilet either from written word or sign, addressing the correct medic or paramedic, recognising who they are by their uniform, other patients who are waiting to be seen, and by knowing that you can communicate your anxiety in an intelligent coherent manner and question where appropriate. There was none of that in this situation and I felt frightened, frustrated and sometimes angry.

Through all this I still needed to comfort, cajole and play with and reassure my son that he was alright and that I wouldn't leave him in the hospital and that he would be able to see his dad later. This was a position difficult to maintain since I had similar needs to his.'

It is difficult for anyone who has never experienced the inability to communicate to appreciate or even begin to understand the feelings of frustration, insecurity, anger and fear for those facing this problem in their day-to-day life. The aim in starting this paper with the experience of this woman is to illustrate precisely the degree of anxiety generated by all those mixed-up emotions particularly when a person is faced with an illness and yet is totally unable to relate or communicate effectively with those believed to be in a position to help.

The woman who related the above story is a competent professional. She is a white middle class woman and therefore has less stresses in life than those faced by working class black women. Yet when faced with the illness of her son in an unfamiliar health service she could neither communicate effectively nor was she able to identify to whom she was trying to communicate by merely looking at the uniform. Her confidence left her and what dominated her emotions was fear and frustration even though she had money and a passport and knew that the nightmare could only be of a week's duration.

Reflecting on the above story this section focuses on black people and black women in particular who must face the problems of communication in their interaction with the health service at both primary and secondary level. What has been their experience?

Consultative Paper number three contained a report on the discussion group of the Somali women. Most of the women in this group do not speak English, their anxieties about the inability to relate or communicate were heightened when they or their relatives were ill and they had to visit a doctor in a surgery or go to a hospital. Some women stated that on many occasions they had to wait for days before they could find someone within the community who could serve as an interpreter during a consultation in hospital or in a surgery/health centre. Interviews with receptionists in a Health Centre suggested that where no interpreter was available hand language was often resorted to. This was confirmed by the women who added that they never understood what the doctor said and they were convinced that the doctor was equally at a loss as to what their complaint was about, and this, as will be seen later, can sometimes have disastrous consequences.

## 1. Interpreting Service — An Evaluation

Following these discussions the Health Service's Race Relations Advisory Committee was approached to find out whether or not there was an interpreting service to help overcome the problem of language at both primary and secondary care level. The Liverpool Health Authority did provide an interpreting service. A list was available to health workers in different departments and it was supposed to be updated twice a year. An evaluation of the service was suggested and questionnaires were sent to all the people on the list. This was done in conjunction and with the full co-operation of the secretary of the Race Relations Advisory Committee. A total of 59 questionnaires were sent.

In the questionnaire a number of areas were covered e.g. where were the interpreters located, as that would determine their availability; which sections of the population needed more interpreters, the sex of the interpreters in relation to that of the patients, etc. It was also thought useful to find out if the interpreters had had any problems in their role and if they had any recommendations on the ways in which the service could be improved.

One respondent pointed out that when she was on duty she could not be available to interpret for patients in other departments. Another respondent suggested that the service could be improved by the recruitment of Chinese interpreters. Most of the interpreters had been part of the service for more than a year, but most of them had been for the French and German languages. This is not surprising since all the interpreters who responded were professionals employed by the Liverpool Health Authority, and there is, as the recent Liverpool Health Authority survey shows, a gross under-representation of racial minorities in this area.

The Health Authority was indeed concerned by the results of this study and attempts were made to recruit more interpreters and indeed the December 1987 up-date was a great improvement on the 1986 version. In addition, the Authority had a list of useful telephone numbers in the event of having to use an interpreter, in an emergency, and the list was made available to different health departments. But even if there were more interpreters in the service, would that effectively meet the needs of those who need an interpreting service?

### a. Results of the Questionnaire

The results of this study were very disappointing in terms of the response rate as well as the information contained in the questionnaires. Of the 59 questionnaires sent out only 12 were completed and returned. Of those, only two were interpreters for black people (one a Yoruba and the other a Hausa). Not surprisingly none of them had been called upon to interpret. Most people from Nigeria do speak English. Not only was this country a British colony but locally resident people from Nigeria tend to be students or professionals in various capacities. In the returned questionnaires there was one interpreter for the Chinese, none for the different Asian languages, the Somalis or the Vietnamese. These are the groups that have expressed great concern in this area. Of all the interpreters, the Welsh interpreter is the only one who appears to have been used consistently, interpreting for two to three patients on a weekly basis. The Chinese interpreter had 10 to 15 patients and the rest had had one or none in the previous twelve months.

*b. The Effectiveness of the Existing Interpreting Service*

There are a number of reasons why the existing interpreting service will not achieve its objectives effectively. Firstly, most of the interpreters are employees of the National Health Service. This is obviously an advantage since they are already familiar with the terminology used in the field of health. But as employees they already have their own jobs to perform and although amongst those who returned the questionnaires only one reported this as a problem, it is known that more interpreters have at times felt that they could not easily leave their work to go and interpret in another department at short notice. One interpreter took her name off the list precisely for that reason. She felt that it was not easy to leave a woman in the middle of a delivery nor was it fair to keep a person who needed an interpreter waiting for that length of time. Secondly employees have time off and therefore cannot provide an effective cover in cases of emergencies. Thirdly, they are located mainly in hospitals and this has two disadvantages: (1) Their existence is not generally known to the people in the community and therefore there will be people like the Somali women who will not go for consultation unless assured that someone will interpret for them. (2) Because of their location they are not easily accessible at primary health care level. This research, though not exhaustive, has revealed that lack of effective communication at this level can lead to disastrous consequences. The following case studies illustrate this point.

## 2. Communication problems

Most of the empirical work in this area centered on the Somali women. This was mainly because of the constant contact the researcher had with this community in the course of collecting material which is presented in Consultative Paper Three.

*a. Case Study 1*

Mrs. X was 29 years old and had had three children. She had missed her period by one month but had no other signs of pregnancy, so she consulted her General Practitioner but there was no one to interpret. The doctor gave her tablets. A day after she started taking the tablets she started bleeding. For three days she had heavy bleeding and the husband had to go for the doctor. The doctor came to the house. He palpated her but did not check her vaginally. She was given more tablets and left still bleeding. On the fifth day a friend happened to call and it was she who called a taxi to take Mrs. X to the hospital where she was admitted for two nights. She had been pregnant.

### b. Case Study 2

Mrs. T was 49 years old and had had no children in the past six years so when she missed her period for two months she assumed that she was starting the menopause. She went to see her doctor to confirm this. She was given tablets. Soon after taking the tablets she started bleeding and for one day she bled heavily. During the night the bleeding was so heavy that at 12 midnight the husband went to the surgery to find the doctor. The receptionist told him she would ring the doctor. The doctor did not come until 7 a.m. and the ambulance was called to take Mrs. T to hospital at 8 a.m. By this time she was weak and almost unconscious. She was admitted for three days, and she had been pregnant. When she left the hospital she was put on iron tablets.

### c. Case Study 3

The practice in the maternity hospital where Mrs. S had her first baby was to ask women whether or not they wanted to breast-feed their babies. The babies who were going to be breast-fed were given water feeds during the first few days before breast milk was fully developed in the mother. Those who were not to be breast-fed were given milk feeds from the outset. Mrs. S wanted to breast-feed her baby but because of language barriers nobody had explained the system to her. In consequence she was very upset when her baby was given water and others given milk. Thinking that the hospital staff had deliberately starved her baby, she went to the kitchen and brought a milk feed for her baby. The ward sister became angry and brought a leaflet asking Mrs. S to choose the type of milk she wanted for her baby. The leaflet was in English and Mrs. S could not read it. This created more tension and frustration with Mrs. S in tears and wanting to go home, and the staff thinking she was incompetent and would not be able to look after the baby at home.

It was not until visiting time that the sister found a Somali man who could interpret for her. She expressed her fears about Mrs. S's ability to look after the baby at home as she seemed undecided about breast-feeding or milk feeds. It was then that both staff and Mrs. S realised that the confusion was created by lack of communication.

### d. Case Study 4

Mrs. H's experience was not as traumatic but still distressing. Towards the end of her pregnancy she visited the clinic as usual, with no one to interpret. On this particular visit the nurse took her upstairs for an induction. She had come unprepared for admission and her family had no idea why she had not come back from the clinic. When her husband came to find out what had happened, he was told that Mrs. H had been informed on her last visit that she would be admitted for induction on that day, but without an interpreter this information was not understood by Mrs. H.

### e. Case Study 5

The case of Mrs. D goes beyond problems of interpreting to the area of understanding how the health service operates. It also highlights problems of communication other than those in the Health Service. Twelve years ago Mrs. D's three year old son was run over by a car and this left him paralysed and totally disabled and dependent on constant care. To date his case has not yet been taken to court even though the driver accepted responsibility. Mrs. D believes that this is because she does not understand how the system operates and she does not speak English well.

In the summer of this year (1987), Mrs. D's mother came to England to see her disabled grandson for the first time. Whilst staying with her daughter she fell ill. Mrs. D's general practitioner looked after her, but when she did not get better he advised the family to consult a specialist and suggested that this could not be done within the National Health Service because Mrs. D's mother was an overseas patient. The specialist advised admission for an operation mentioning his fee of £550 (including consultation) but not elaborating on the fees for the other five days. Mrs. D's mother was admitted, operated on and was discharged after five days. It was not until Mrs. D received the following bill that she found out how much she had to pay for her mother's hospitalisation:

| | |
|---|---|
| Consultation fee | £ 50.00 |
| Operation fee | £500.00 |
| Anaesthetist fee | £150.00 |
| Radiographic examination | £100.00 |
| X-rays/ECG | £ 75.00 |
| Laboratory fees | £158.00 |
| Blood test | £ 33.00 |

| | |
|---|---|
| Chemist Account | £153.00 |
| Albuminar/Plasma | £146.00 |
| Operation Room | £230.00 |
| Hospital Board | £475.00 |

Around the time of consultation Mrs. D's husband was run over by a car and he died before reaching hospital. Mrs. D was not only having the tragedy of losing her husband but was also left facing a bill of over £2,000. But if Mrs. D's mother had gone to a National Health Service hospital as an overseas patient she would have had the same operation, stayed the same number of days but only paid £870. Within the National Health Service overseas patients pay £174, or £158 if sharing the room for a night but do not pay any extras i.e. surgeon's fee, tests etc. But Mrs. D did not know how the system operated and there was no one to advise her, hence she has ended up with a bill of over £2,000.

Looking at the results of the questionnaires to which the interpreters responded, one might be led to believe that there is not a lot of demand for interpreters in the Health Service in Liverpool. This, as will be seen later from evidence in the Chinese community, is a mistaken view. It is true, as some have argued, that the numbers of racial minorities in Liverpool are lower than those to be found in other parts of the country. Certain cities in the Midlands and certain boroughs in London have larger numbers of racial minorities. But this does not mean that Liverpool does not need to provide an interpreting service.

In a study of the Liverpool black elderly people it was estimated that there are between 20,000 and 30,000 black and ethnic minority people in Liverpool. Table 18 gives a breakdown of the different racial groups.

As the table shows, there is a substantial number of people whose first language is not English. It is true that not all of them are unable to speak English, but most of those who do speak English tend to be men rather than women and it is the latter who for a variety of reasons use the Health Service more frequently. It is also important to draw a distinction between speaking a language and being able to communicate effectively in that medium. In the course of the present Health Project contact has been made with some racial minority women who do speak English but who feel that the level at which they speak the language is not sufficient for effective communication with health

Table 18   Estimate of Liverpool's Black Population 1981

| Group | Estimate | | % |
|---|---|---|---|
| | Min. | Max. | |
| British Black | 7,400 | 11,100 | 37 |
| Chinese | 3,000 | 4,500 | 15 |
| West Indian | 2,600 | 3,900 | 13 |
| Arab | 2,600 | 3,900 | 13 |
| African | 2,400 | 3,600 | 12 |
| Asian | 2,000 | 3,000 | 10 |
| TOTAL | 20,000 | 30,000 | 100 |

(Source: Barney Rooney, *Racism and Resistance to Change: A Study of the Black Social Workers Project*, Liverpool Social Services Department, 1987).

workers. The same problem has been expressed by some health workers interviewed who find it difficult to put across medical information to people whose knowledge of English is limited. The extent of need for interpreters has been fully demonstrated in the Chinese community.

The Pagoda, a Chinese Community Centre, had two part-time workers who were funded by Manpower Services Commission (MSC). There was also a full-time worker who was an employee of the City Council. Part of the work for the employees was interpreting for the Chinese in their interaction with the various departments in the city. The Pagoda keeps statistics on their interpreting service and in the month of October 1987, they interpreted for 165 people in the Health Service. Roughly 40% of those were hospital based and 60% were with general practitioners. These statistics are an indication that there is a need for an interpreting service in Liverpool not just for the Chinese but for all those who cannot communicate effectively in English. This, as the table shows, relates to the Arabs, Africans, and Asians.

Discussions with one of the interpreters in the Pagoda revealed that there are a number of problems faced by workers in this area. One concerns waiting time. On many occasions hospitals have asked for their services and yet made no attempt to get the patients seen as soon as the interpreter arrives. In some cases interpreters have been made to wait for up to three hours. This is an unacceptable situation since they have other duties to perform in the community. But even if the interpreter has come with a patient from the community the length of time spent in one hospital could determine whether or not other appointments for interpreting in other institutions can be kept. A former interpreter recalled instances of frustration as she tried in vain to keep interpreting appointments in two different hospitals.

The other problem relates to parking space. Interpreters spend a lot of time trying to find parking at both hospitals and surgeries/health centres. In one particular health centre, a doctor objected to anyone using doctors' parking space even though such spaces were not being used at the time.

## 3. Recommendations

It is obvious that there are a number of problems with the Health Authority voluntary interpreting service and that something needs to be done to improve the service. Recruiting more interpreters, as the Health Authority is doing, is a good starting point. But this in itself is unlikely to solve the problems. Even if the numbers were increased significantly and they remained voluntary interpreters, this would still pose problems. The Health Service has a statutory obligation to provide a service and in that capacity it cannot rely on voluntary workers to carry out its duties. There is, therefore, a need for an interpreting service that is based on paid workers who could be called upon whenever needed. This cannot be done effectively with voluntary workers.

Within the Health Service voluntary interpreters are already employed in their respective departments and as has been stated it is not always possible for these workers to leave their jobs and go and interpret elsewhere. Within the Health Service, therefore, there is a need to have paid workers whose specific work is to interpret. If they are located in hospitals or health centres they will be easily accessible during emergencies.

In addition, and even more urgent, is a need to have interpreters based in the community and being known to those who need their service. The results at the Pagoda Centre give strong evidence in support of this recommendation. Not only would such interpreters be known to the community but they would also be acceptable since they would be drawn from the respective communities. As paid members of the Health Service they would be bound by the same principle of confidentiality and therefore would not discuss patients' illnesses outside their role of interpreting.

The advantage of having health professionals as interpreters has been referred to already, i.e. the knowledge of the terminology used in the Health Service. It is suggested that for interpreters without this knowledge, some form of training will be necessary. The training should go beyond just interpreting to include giving information on how the Health Service operates as well as teaching workers the basics of health promotion and preventative health care.

The work done by the interpreters in the Pagoda Centre shows that there is a demand for this service in various sectors in the city. It would make financial sense therefore to establish a network of interpreters who will be paid from funds pooled from these sectors. This could mean the Health Service, the Family Practitioner Committee and the City Council and other sectors working jointly to establish such a network. Some of the workers should be based in community centres, e.g. Pagoda, Pakistan, Somali, etc. and others in Health Centres and hospitals, and there should be an overall organiser who will facilitate liaison between all workers in the interpreting service.

Finally the Health Service needs to look at ways of easing the problems of interpreters by arranging its appointment system bearing in mind the need to provide interpreters in certain cases. Discussion on these problems with interpreters would be helpful. Similarly there is a need to look at the parking arrangements for interpreters when called in for emergencies. This paper highlights the problems inherent in the Health Service voluntary interpreting service but it is hoped it does more than that. It is hoped that the report raises the whole question of the relations between the Health Service and the black community in Liverpool, and that link will be the subject of the next paper when the area of mental health is considered.

# Mental Health

## 1. A General Overview

This paper looks at Black people and mental illness, but first the concept of mental illness and the role of psychiatry are discussed. This is an essential starting point as it is only in the light of what is known or unknown about mental illness in general that it is possible to evaluate critically what professionals have to say about Black people in this field.

For many years the sociology of mental illness has remained a controversial issue. The major dispute among students of mental illness has been over the meaning of the concept, and about what actually is meant by the assertion that a person is mentally ill. Why do some people develop symptoms of mental illness and others not? It is in an attempt to answer these questions that various schools of thought have arisen. Some of these approaches are examined here: the psychiatric, the labelling and the social control perspectives.

To the adherents of the psychiatric perspective, represented in the works of Spitzer[1] and Wing,[2] mental illness is regarded as a disease in the same category as any other physical illness. The assumption made is that in mental illness there is some form of neurological defect responsible for the disordered form of thinking and behaviour. Within this school, psychiatry itself is defined as 'a medical speciality concerned with the study, diagnosis, and treatment of mental illness'.[3] As a branch of medicine therefore, psychiatry uses a similar model in defining mental illness as that used by medical practitioners. In physical illness, 'the norm is the structural and functional integrity of the human body', and a person is defined ill when there is a deviation from this norm.[4] What then, in the field of psychiatry, is the norm, deviation from which is regarded as mental illness? This is the question asked by among others, Scheff[5] and Szasz[6] who are proponents of the labelling theory. They do not subscribe to the view that there is any scientific ground upon which to draw parallels between medicine as such and psychiatry. According to Szasz, there is no such thing as mental illness. Mental illness, he asserts:

'is a myth which only exists in the same way as do other theoretical concepts, and yet, to those who believe in them, familiar theories are likely to appear, sooner or later, as "objective truths" or "facts".'[7]

But by asserting that mental illness is a myth Szasz does not deny the existence of personal unhappiness and socially deviant behaviour. He argues, however, that this is not physical illness in which the body-functioning violates anatomical and physiological norms. The mentally ill are only so defined

'when their personal conduct violates certain ethical and social norms. Hence the labelling as mentally ill of such historical figures as Jesus, Hitler, Job and Castro.'[8]

The assertion Szasz makes finds support in the ways in which psychiatry has been used to enforce social and political conformity. A recent BBC2 programme, *A Secret World of Sex* (April 23rd 1991) revealed that under the 1913 Mental Defectives Act, 10,000 young women in England were committed to asylums for having sex before marriage. One such woman, Edna Higginbottom, who was given electric shock treatment, was shut away for 20 years and was only released in 1959 when the Act was repealed.

In Western Society the most written about example is the plight of political dissidents in Russia. It was the alleged abuse of psychiatry which led to the expulsion of the Soviet Society of Psychiatrists from the World Psychiatric Association six years ago.[9] Not only were dissidents labelled mentally ill, but according to Dr. Glutzman, himself a dissident, they were also subjected to punitive treatment:

'. . . if a patient is found with a pen or piece of paper in his possession, he is immediately given one month's treatment of sulfazine.'[10]

This drug was not given for therapeutic reasons but specifically to induce 'severe pain, fever and muscle necrosis'.[11]

Although Russia has been singled out as the offender, media coverage and reports of what happens to prisoners of conscience in countries outside the Soviet suggest that the abuse of psychiatry is not restricted to the Soviet Union. Nor is the label of mental illness only used to discredit political opponents. In its subtle form it is a tool used by institutions to undermine individuals who stand up to authority. This is easily done by casting doubt about the stability of the individual's mental state. Once the state of mind has been questioned one's confidence wanes and doubts about one's own behaviour begin to creep in. This is the most effective way of destroying insubordinate members within organisations which still want to maintain their image of being just and caring. The self-fulfilling prophecy syndrome leaves the individual open to being officially labelled mentally ill.

But as Szasz points out, there have never been any objective truth or predictable laws which demonstrate the validity of labelling certain people mentally ill. The history of psychiatry begins with the building of asylums for the insane which started in France in the seventeenth century and gradually spread over the whole of Europe. Among those imprisoned in these institutions were not only the so-called mad but also 'abandoned children, prostitutes, incurably sick persons, the aged and the indigent'.[12] These groups constituted the 'undesirables' of society and putting them in asylums was a way of removing them from society and controlling their movement. This incarceration of innocent people was rationalised:

> 'by means of the imagery and rhetoric of madness, insanity, psychosis, schizophrenia, mental illness – call it what you will – which transformed the inmate into a "patient", his prison into a "hospital" and warden into a "doctor".'[13]

The transition, however, has not altered the role psychiatry still plays in society – that of stigmatising social undesirables as mentally ill. There are of course differences, as Szasz points out, between the conduct of a depressed person and that of a contented and even-tempered individual, just as there are differences between the conduct of people who are under delusions and that of those who are not so deluded. But the differences do not arise as a result of a diseased mind but rather as a response to what Szasz calls 'problems in living' which include 'conflicting personal needs, opinions, social aspirations, values and so forth'. Szasz's objection to the use of psychiatric diagnostic terms in this area is because such terms are used:

> 'to stigmatize, dehumanize, imprison and torture those to whom they are applied ... Words such as insane, mad, psychotic, depressed, suicidal, mentally ill, and others have long been used, and continue to be used, to justify involuntary psychiatric interventions.'[14]

The other question asked by the adherents of the labelling perspective is why certain individuals and not others are selected to take on the role of mentally ill person. Scheff argues that what are regarded as symptoms of mental illness are widespread in the population, but many people displaying such symptoms are never categorised as being out of their minds. Scheff's observation finds support in an anecdote about Isaac Newton, the scientist, famous for his discovery of the force of gravity. In order to allow his beloved cat free access into the house without disturbing his concentration, he made a hole in the door. But this cosy arrangement was disrupted when the cat produced nine kittens. But the genius had a prompt solution to the problem: nine little holes in the door. Nobody suggested he was out of his mind. It was seen as the case of 'the absent-minded genius'. The veracity of the story is not relevant here but an important point is being made. In general, people in society are quite happy to make allowances for the eccentricities of people with status or power but are quick to label those of people without such attributes as mentally ill. This is why Scheff asserts that it is not the behaviour as such but rather the social response to individuals which is the major determinant of whether such persons will be labelled mentally ill or not.[15] Once so labelled, individuals take on the role of the mentally ill and conform to the stereotyped expectations of how they are supposed to behave. In this context the labelling of individuals as mentally ill is viewed as a form of social control and, as Horwitz[16] points out, it is this aspect of mental health which has attracted the attention of many sociologists such as Goffman,[17] Stanton and Schwartz,[18] Hollingshead and Redlich[19] and many others. The researchers in these studies, as Horwitz points out, were not particularly concerned with a general theory of social control but the questions raised remain central to the study of mental illness as a form of social control. Horwitz, who is the proponent of the social control theory, gives a summary of the questions raised in these studies:

'1. Under what conditions is mental illness, rather than some other label, used to categorize behaviour?
2. When will observers label or deny that someone is mentally ill?
3. How does the attribution of mental illness vary by the social class, ethnic identification, gender, and other characteristics of the labeller and labellee?
4. After people have been labelled mentally ill, what factors predict the type of social response accorded them?

5. What circumstances are associated with the variation in the amount and type of psychotherapy provided to the mentally ill?'[20]

These questions are relevent also in the field of race and mental health since it is believed by many that in Britain the labelling of racial minorities as mentally ill is a form of social control.

To exponents of a social control perspective mental illness refers to:

'a category that observers use to classify particular individuals, not to the symptoms these individuals display. The concept of mental illness is located in observers' categories rather than in actors' symptoms.'[21]

Horwitz asserts that when observers perceive that the behaviour is 'incomprehensible', that is it lacks reason, purpose or intent, they will then label such behaviour as mental illness. This remains so regardless of 'the particular cultural or historical setting'.[22] In this way Horwitz posits a universal concept of mental illness which has been strongly questioned by the relativist theorists who argue for cultural relativity in the definition and treatment of mental illness. Benedict, for example, points out that people who might be labelled mad in one society because of the behaviour they exhibit may be considered quite sane in another society.[23] Others have, as has been illustrated in the anecdote above, argued that within one society the perception of mental illness and the treatment given to those so perceived is determined by the class of the individuals. In their study, Hollingshead and Redlich found that classes I to IV were under-represented in the mentally ill patient population when compared to the general population. But as their figures show Class V was over-represented in the patient population.

Table 19   Class Status and the Distribution of Patients and Non-Patients in the Population

| | Population% | |
| Class | Patients | Non-Patients |
| --- | --- | --- |
| I | 1.0 | 3.0 |
| II | 7.0 | 8.4 |
| III | 13.7 | 20.4 |
| IV | 40.1 | 49.8 |
| V | 38.2 | 18.4 |

Hollingshead & Redlich, 1958, p. 199.

From the above statistics the authors conclude that 'the distribution of patients in comparison to non-patients by class is significant'.[24] Their conclusion lends support to Magaro's view on the analysis of the cultural context of madness.

Central to Magaro's analysis is the view that the definition of mental illness and who is so afflicted has always been within the context of the dominant cultural ideology of the time. Taking a historical perspective he traces the process by means of which the bourgeoisie achieved ascendancy, and how the accompanying dominant ideology led to the emergence of two forms of treatment for the mentally ill. In France, Magaro states, Pinel, a psychiatrist, led the development of institutions for treating the poor amongst whom the symptom for being mentally ill was lack of self-control, a characteristic already attributed to the lower classes. Treatment embodied the morality of the middle classes and it was aimed at eliciting remorse and guilt from which would come the desire by the poor classes to incorporate the values of society. Included in the behaviour which indicated failure to respond to treatment were:

> 'disobedience, theft, and resistance to work, the three horsemen of a bourgeoisie society.'[25]

Those who refused to work, obey or continued to steal remained confined to the dungeons of the asylums. Conformity was the mark of cure, behaviour had to reflect the dominant morality of the bourgeois society. This was true of Tuke's treatment of the lower middle classes in England. Mad individuals were seen as being in need only of moral guidance to learn the proper behaviour. Work was the main treatment as a means of providing a moral rule, a submission to a higher order and an engagement of responsibility. As part of the treatment Tuke's patients were invited to tea and dinner parties. On these occasions they were expected to dress in their fineries and exhibit the proper manners and accepted social customs. For those who conformed and exhibited acceptable behaviour, a cure was claimed. Both Pinel and Tuke in their professional capacity acted as agents of the dominant class in society and the desired effect of their work was to incorporate to the dominant culture the poor who were perceived as deviants; hence the mental illness label, and the confinement in asylums, when this incorporation was resisted.

But, asks Magaro, how was madness defined and treated when it affected the controllers of society – the educated middle and upper classes? Lack of self-control was not the symptom of madness in this group since the middle classes were already perceiving themselves as strong-willed. Their affliction was seen as the result of materialism and treatment was directed at the encouragement of non-materialism. In addition the affliction of the middle classes with mental illness was seen as the result of the influence of astrological events. Mesmer, the mentor in this field, explained how people's lives were influenced by the stars which controlled the flowing of the magnetic fluid which filled the universe:

> 'The harmony of this fluid within the individual protected against disease, hence, treatment was achieving the necessary balance by controlling the flow of fluid. The treatment object was a banquet, an arrangement of mirrors and rods, which directed the magnetic flow to the individual.'[26]

Marago's argument here is that the dominant section in society dictates what is mental illness, who should be defined as ill, and what treatment should be administered. The definers in almost all situations are those who wield power and therefore are in a position to construe what is social reality. This was true in the past and it remains true to this day, hence Marago's observation that:

> 'the imposition of the middle class belief system on others under the guise of treatment remains with us until today.'[27]

From Magaro's analysis there is no suggestion that the definers of mental illness were not familiar with the culture of the people they were labelling as mentally ill. On the contrary, they were fully aware of the differences between their value system and that of the poor classes. It was therefore not an action based on ignorance but on the evaluation of a culture which was perceived as inferior, deviant and sick. The significance of this point will be elaborated when the role of multi-culturalism in the field of race and mental health is discussed. This brief discussion shows how controversial are the issues involved in the definition of mental illness and its treatment. The work of the researchers who have contributed to the analysis of mental illness among racial minorities is now considered. The consensus in this field is that black people are more mentally ill than white people. Given the fact that there is no agreement on what constitutes mental illness what yardstick is used to measure the degree of madness among black people?

## 2. Black people and Mental Illness

Looking back in history it is evident that psychiatry has had a prominent role in explaining the experience of black people. During the era of slavery, for example, 'drapetomania' was diagnosed as a mental illness peculiar to slaves. Its main characteristic was 'the irresistible urge to run away from the plantation'.[28] This 'scientific' definition in the behaviour of slaves no doubt provided a justification and a rationalisation for keeping such individuals in chains, as well as for the atrocities committed by some slave-catchers which included the chopping off of part of the slave's foot to slow down the running away process.[29]

The days of imperialism witnessed a widened scope in the use of psychiatry as a means of justifying forced rule over the colonials by pointing to the inferiority and immaturity of the mind of the ruled. Even the revolt against such rule, as in the case of the Mau Mau uprising, was explained as recently as the 1950s in terms of the infantility of the Kikuyu people, an indication that they are still in need of firm direction by their superiors – the whites.[30]

The settlement of black people in Britain from the 1950s onwards provided an opportunity to study them at closer quarters. The general conclusion reached by most researchers was that black people are more prone to mental illness when compared to the indigenous white population. There is, however, no consensus as to why this should be the case. One reason put forward for the observed higher rates is migration per se. It is suggested that the movement of people from rural Third World countries to an urban environment in the Western world is bound to have psychological effects on the migrants.

In his study in the East End of London Gordon looked at 112 West Indian patients admitted over a period of three years in Long Grove Hospital, Epsom. His explanation for the high rates of mental illness among this group was in terms of 'cultural stress reactions'; the main stress being environmental, namely acculturation.[31] He supports his findings by referring to previous studies carried out by Murphy on refugees in Britain[32] and Malzberg et al on immigrant Negroes in New York State.[33] Kiev, in a study of patients attending a group general practice in Brixton, reached a similar conclusion. West Indians had a higher rate of conspicuous psychiatric morbidity as a group compared to the English patients. His study, he concluded:

'pointed to definite sources of strain in the West Indian community in London associated with a shift from the agricultural and pastoral

life of the West Indies to the strenuous demands of a highly indus-
trialized urban society.'[34]

Similar assertions are to be found in the conclusions made by Hensi[35]
and Mashmi[36] who found higher rates of mental breakdown among
the black immigrants.

It was Burke who drew attention to conditions existing in the host
country which may have an impact on the mental health of the
migrants. In a study conducted between 1962 and 1972 he found
lower rates of attempted suicides among Asians in comparison with
the native Britons. But within the Asian community there were differences between men and women – the latter with a rate twice as high as
the former, which suggests:

'that language difficulties may be important in the adjustment of
female immigrants in foreign environments.'[37]

Burke's findings find support in a later study by Schofield in which
she points to isolation as a major part of the lives of many Asian
women, and language difficulties as a factor which compounds this
feeling of isolation. Muslim women in particular remain at home and
therefore get lonely and depressed. Schofield, however, included in
her assessment other social factors such as racial harassment and
general racial disadvantage.[38]

That migration per se is not the only factor responsible for mental
disorders is a point made by Hitch and Rack in their study of Polish
and Ukrainian refugees in psychiatric hospitals in Bradford. The
former showed a higher first admission rate than did the Ukrainians
and this was because the 'Poles are often socially secluded from the
host population and also from fellow nationals' and this 'enhances a
marginal identity'.[39]

Cochrane found no justification for seeing immigrants as a group
whose mental illness can be explained within the context of migration. In his study he found that Asian children had lower rates of
behavioural deviance and mental hospital admission when compared
to British children, whereas the West Indian children showed similar
rates to those of English children but had higher rates of admission to
mental hospitals. The pattern for adults follows that noted for children.[40] There are others, however, who see the lower rate among the
Asian population as a reflection of the under-utilisation of services
rather than relatively good mental health. Brewin, for example, points
to the existence of lay healers as alternatives to Western psychiatric

services and suggests that the 200 hakims present in Britain may be providing this service.[41] Nevertheless, Cochrane's observations prompted others to look further into differences between the immigrant groups to account for variations. National and racial differences were thought to be important.

The selection hypothesis suggested the pre-existence of abnormalities which might lie behind the impulse to migrate and the fact that immigrants are more likely to break down under the stress of migration. Bebbington *et al* who found high rates of severe functional disorder among the West Indian immigrants thus concluded that studies seeking to provide a theoretical explanation for any association found between immigration and mental disorders must also take into account other relative factors such as race, cultural background, reasons for and intentions in migration, to which countries and with what consequences.[42]

The selection hypothesis moved the 'problem' back to the country of origin by suggesting that certain individuals may have been mentally ill even before they left their own countries. The acceptance of this theory within the medical profession is perhaps reflected in the statement made by Dr Sklar to the Brent Community Health Council:

'They are slightly neurotic. It is difficult to say whether they are more neurotic in this country or where they have come from. To get the right answer you would have to practise there.'[43]

What Sklar is suggesting is not, however, a novel idea. Anthropologists have customarily studied black people in their 'own environment' and brought back reports to support theories held about black people. This practice is now encouraged among those with an interest in the health of racial minorities.

So far the studies discussed above have tended to focus on migration as a possible cause of mental illness albeit with others pointing to the possibility that different factors may be implicated. Other studies, however, have isolated as the cause the culture of the people who are seen to be exhibiting symptoms of mental illness.

Kiev noted among the 150 West Indians he interviewed religious delusions which he believed to be rooted in the West Indian culture. He concluded that culture was influential on the form and content of mental illness and, according to him, the high level of schizophrenia among this group is culturally determined.[44] Other authors have also noted persecutory delusions among immigrants; Copeland among his West African patients,[45] Gordon among West Indians[46] and Carpenter and Brockington among West Indians, Asians and Africans living in Manchester. The authors in the Manchester study state that their subjects had delusions 'especially delusions of persecution . . . which suggest paranoid psychosis rather than true schizophrenia'.[47]

The high risk among the immigrant population of developing psychosis was also noted by a British Medical Journal editorial which pointed to high rates of paranoia in the ethnic group to which the immigrant belongs, selective migration of those already prone to develop psychosis, and the short-term stress of living in an alien social environment, as explanations for this high risk. But it also pointed to one factor which it stated was rarely mentioned – misdiagnosis by experts who belong to a different culture, and concluded that:

> 'Misdiagnosis could, indeed, be an important factor in accounting for the high prevalence of psychosis found in West Indians, Asians and Africans.'[48]

This recognition of cultural differences is the line taken by the adherents of transcultural psychiatry. This is now an influential viewpoint in psychiatry.

Most medical professionals would now accept that a highly sophisticated level of cultural knowledge is an essential prerequisite to effective diagnosis and treatment of mental illness. Where such knowledge is lacking there is a danger of a breakdown in communication between the patient and those who provided the services. This may lead to wrong diagnosis and unnecessarily prolonged stay in mental institutions. It is for this reason that Cox asserts that:

> 'the treatment of a patient from a contrasting culture is a transcultural dyadic, and for communication to be meaningful the psychiatrist may need not only to understand his own prejudices but also to accept certain modifications and limitations of his customary clinical style.'[49]

The emphasis in this approach is for psychiatrists and general practitioners to be aware not only of different cultures but also of the different ways in which members of such cultures present their symptoms of illness generally. Ballard, for example, stresses how easy it is for an observer outside a cultural system to dismiss its ideas as misguided. When the providers do not understand the code being used by the patient, the communication 'may seem bizarre and deluded, evidence perhaps of schizophrenia'.[50] There is indeed enough evidence to suggest that more often than not black people when seen by psychiatrists are diagnosed as suffering from schizo-phrenia. A Bradford hospital study showed that more immigrants from the New Commonwealth were diagnosed as schizophrenic when compared with the indigenous white population.[51] Similarly, in Nottingham, 29% of notified schizophrenic patients were from racial minorities and yet this group only accounted for 6.5% of the city's population.[52] This lack of cultural knowledge has also been identified by researchers in Liverpool.

In Liverpool, for example, a psychiatrist informed us of a West Indian patient who was diagnosed as psychotic and placed in a mental hospital on the basis that he expressed as his ultimate aim in life a desire to get his people to their God in Africa.[53] The psychiatrist and the social worker involved with the patient knew nothing about Rastafarianism and they made no effort to find out about it as part of their general inquiry as to how mentally ill their patient was. This is not an isolated case. Another case which attracted the national press is that of Steve Thompson who on refusing to have his Rasta locks shorn was diagnosed as schizophrenic and was in consequence transferred to Rampton security hospital a few weeks before he was released from Gartree Prison.[54] Thompson's release, three months after his commit-tal to Rampton under Section 72 of the Mental Health Act of 1959, was the result of the reports from an independent group of psychiatrists, one of them a West Indian, who argued that Thompson was not displaying the kind of mental illness which warranted admission into Rampton.[55]

The central question which arises from the Thompson case is this: was a West Indian psychiatrist included in the team of people who made the initial diagnosis on the basis of which Thompson was committed to Rampton? This is not to say that all black psychiatrists have a deep appreciation of different cultures when dealing with patients. In fact there is enough support for the view that many black health workers trained in Western medicine and coming from a middle class background tend to share the same attitude as their white counterparts.[56] What is argued here, however, is that a West Indian psychiatrist would be more likely to know what Rastafarianism means even if she/he personally did not subscribe to, or believe in that particular religion, and hence should have the ability to assess what is mental illness and what is cultural belief. It is for this reason that Rack, one of the most outstanding proponents of the transcultural approach, stresses the need to include racial minority professionals in the clinical team as part of diagnosing and treating psychiatric patients:

'The best interpreter is one with whom one works regularly, who gets to know the meaning and significance of the questions one is asking; in fact, not just a linguistic technician but a member of the clinical team. It is fashionable these days to talk about multi-disciplinary teams. I believe that in treating patients with a different language and culture, a team approach is essential, and it should be not only multi-disciplinary but multi-ethnic.'[57]

To summarise: the explanations for the alleged high rate of mental illness among black people as put forward in the work of the various researchers fall under one of the following categories:

1) Migration per se causes mental illness.
2) The people affected by the migration process are those who were already unstable in their countries of origin (selection hypothesis).
3) The culture of the people is responsible, as in the case of schizophrenia among the West Indians.
4) It is lack of understanding of the immigrant culture by the experts which leads to misdiagnosis (the transculturalists' argument).

Referring back to the concept of mental illness discussed above, it would appear that some of the explanations tend to lean towards Szasz's interpretation which sees what is defined as mental illness as a response to 'problems in living'. The problem as defined by the experts is therefore a psycho-social one and yet the treatment is guided by the psychiatric perspective in which a remedy is sought in terms of drugs and electro-convulsive therapy. As Szasz points out:

'The definition of the disorder and the terms in which its remedy is sought are therefore at odds with one another. The practical significance of this covert conflict between the alleged nature of the defect and the remedy can hardly be exaggerated.'[58]

But even more interesting is the assumption made in these studies about black people as an 'immigrant' group. As early as 1978 social scientists such as Little were already stressing the myth of such an assumption:

'45% of the black community in this country were born here. By the end of this century ... 65% or 70% of the black and brown communities will have been born here . . . this is the first idea to put absolutely at the centre of public, political and professional attention.'[59]

In sea-ports such as Liverpool, London or Bristol where black people have been settled for centuries, it is not just a question of first generation but second, third and even fourth. Their 'mental' or 'neurotic' condition cannot be explained in terms of cultural adjustment or even cultural background since their culture is now 'British', and any mental illness among this group should be assessed within the context of the British culture in which they are a part and within which they have to cope with 'problems in living'. And just what is perceived as a major problem in living in England as far as black people are concerned? The answer for the majority of black people is racism. The extent and the pervasiveness of racism in British society is a factor now acknowledged by a substantial number of white people as well, and yet in the majority of studies which pointed to changes in the environment, racism was not even seen as part of that new environment.

The centrality of racism has been the subject of a variety of papers published recently under the title of 'Racism and Mental Illness'. The editor stresses the importance of racism:

> '. . . from the psychological point of view racism is the singular most important issue of our time. It surpasses poverty simply because it causes that poverty. Indeed in the last two centuries this racism had grown to become an integral part of European culture to lead to the devastation of many and to become an inevitable bugbear of populations which now bear the scars of this evil force.'[60]

The transculturalists have indeed moved a step forward in recognising the possibility of misdiagnosing because the practitioners are not familiar with the culture of their patient, hence their call for multiculturalism in the diagnosis and treatment of mentally ill patients. It is maintained, however, that even this progressive thought as exemplified in the work of Rack still misses the point. It is not so much lack of knowledge about the culture of black people that is the problem but the evaluation of that culture within a dominant white ideological setting which has been conditioned by centuries of racism starting from slavery through imperialism to the Immigration Acts. Different cultures in themselves are not a problem. The problem arises when the superiority of white culture is assumed and other cultures perceived and treated as deviant and bizarre to the extent of labelling those who belong to them as psychotic or schizophrenic. This is not to say that all National Health Service personnel are racist in dealing with racial minorities. They are not, at least not consciously. Many health workers would claim to hold anti-racist views. But in cultural terms the subconscious is often influenced by what is known and accepted as the 'norm'. In this sense, even those who are not explicitly racist may still accept a narrow vision of British culture as the norm and this acceptance informs the way they relate to other cultures. This all embracing cultural racism is noted by Hartman and Husband when they write:

> 'Racist beliefs and imagery are culturally ubiquitous and the historical implications of skin colour which are part of the cultural legacy of all Britons constitute a potential basis of perception and action. This is why it can be quite misleading to label people as prejudiced or unprejudiced as though prejudice were a purely personal characteristic, present in some people and absent in others; and largely a matter of individual morality or pathology. Prejudice resides in the culture. People differ in the degree to which prejudiced cultural assumptions rather than egalitarian assumptions enter into their perspectives on the world and underlie their actions; but the root assumptions are the familiar property of all.'[61]

In his later work Husband reiterates this point. Racism, he argues, takes on 'different nuances in different sub-cultures' but it nevertheless remains common to a white British consciousness. Even those who claim not to be racists find themselves enveloped in this all-embracing, perhaps unconscious, racism which nevertheless leads them to the formulation of or support for theories which have in themselves racist implications. It is perhaps not surprising to find that liberal thinkers such as Rack are at the same time lending support to notions of repatriation. He is, of course, recommending this as a form of 'therapy' for certain patients. Indeed, as he stresses, he may not be 'concerned with repatriation as social policy, as advocated by certain political groups'.[63] But neither did researchers who recommended that Asians should change their culture and diet in order to avoid rickets have any 'conscious' concern about the desires of the explicit cultural racists who feel that 'when in Rome do as the Romans do'. In the absence of evidence suggesting that repatriation is in the interest of the patient and that it is a reliable form of therapy in terms of recovery, Rack's recommendation has little to differentiate it from that of 'certain political groups' which simply want to get rid of people diagnosed as mentally ill. Rack himself refers to the work of Burke[64] and Mahy.[65] The two authors looked at the patients in Jamaica who had been repatriated from Britain. Both researchers came to the conclusion that repatriation was not to be recommended, since those who were repatriated did not only remain ill but were also isolated, since their relatives, believing that they were a 'failure', were not welcoming to them. Rack is, however, reluctant to accept such conclusions and finds them 'somewhat disingenuous' because:

'these findings cannot tell us anything about the successful ones who have avoided further contact with psychiatric services . . .'[66]

Rack may not indeed know the benefits of repatriation but he is not ignorant about certain facts which should make anyone who claims to have in mind the interests of black people refrain from giving a professional recommendation of repatriation. He knows, for example, from the work of Gordon,[67] Hemsi[68] and Mayh,[69] that the majority of black people developed mental illness after their arrival in Britain. Having worked in Bradford which has a substantial population of black people he must also be aware of the 'problems of living' faced by the black population and not least of those problems is racism. He is also aware that among his colleagues there are those who will continue to misdiagnose despite his warning about 'cultural pitfalls in the recognition' of certain mental illnesses. Once labelled, such people can be forcefully ejected from the country through Section 90 of the Mental Health Act of 1959, and mental illness is one of the reasons for excluding people from entering Britain. Given the present climate where there is a call for repatriation on a voluntary or non-voluntary basis, and a drive to contain and depoliticize black resistance, is it not possible that Rack's recommendation may give 'scientific objectivity' to the racism perpetrated by his explicitly racist compatriots? These questions, one might think, would be uppermost to professionals, particularly to the liberal transculturalists such as Rack.

It is not surprising that, to many black people, there is little to choose between the repressive agencies and the 'caring' professions. The latter are considered even more dangerous because the experts present themselves as serving the interest of racial minorities. But in fact, consciously or not, what they are doing is to support the arguments of racists, and their support has a considerable weight because they claim 'scientific objectivity'. They provide a rationalisation for the racist actions of the police, the prisons, the courts and social workers when they label black people mentally ill. To some black people there is indeed little point in thinking that the transcultural sector of psychiatry may have members who are not aware of their racism because 'for all their concern about "misunderstanding" black people', they do not 'see race or class as issues which condition or structure people's lives'.[70] Is the race and class blindness part of their job description to which they must adhere? Szasz, taking a general view on the role of psychiatrists, calls for a distinction to be made between two types of physicians:

> 'those who heal, not so much because they are saints, but because that is their job; and those who harm, not so much because they are sinners, but because that is their job. And if some doctors harm – torture rather than treat, murder the soul rather than minister to the body – that is, in part, because society, through the state, asks them, and pays them, to do so. We saw it happen in Nazi Germany, and we hanged many of the doctors. We see it happen in the Soviet Union, and we denounce the doctors with righteous indignation. But when will we see that the same things are happening in the so-called free societies? When will we recognise – and publicly identify – the medical criminals among us? Or is the very possibility of perceiving many of our leading psychiatrists and psychiatric institutions in this way precluded by the fact that they represent the officially correct views and practices?'[71]

In the 1980s more concern has been expressed about the increase in the number of black people who are detained in psychiatric units. A Channel Four documentary programme, 'Bandung File', gave depressing statistics:

1. Black people were three times more likely to be admitted in psychiatric hospitals than white people.
2. 8% of white people were under compulsory admission and the figure for black people was 25%.
3. A quarter of black people under compulsory admission were young Afro-Caribbean men believed to be suffering from one or other of the following psychotic conditions:

   (a) Cannabis psychosis.
   (b) West Indian psychosis.
   (c) Acute psychotic reaction.
   (d) Manic depression.
   (e) Schizophrenia.
4. Whereas 53% of white patients were diagnosed as psychotic the figure for black people was 70%.
5. Black people were twenty-five times more likely to enter psychiatric units through a court order than white people.

6. A third of black people were referred by the police under section 136 of the Mental Health Act.

7. 38% of white people were given major tranquillizers as opposed to 59% black people.[72]

A recent study by Harris (1988) confirms the findings of the Bandung File programme and points to a substantial increase in the rates for schizophrenia among the 'second generation' British born Afro-Caribbeans.[73] Harris refers to other studies which have produced similar results to his own. Sinclair *et al* (1988) found that for Afro-Caribbean British born males between 16 and 44 years the rate for schizophrenia was 16.67 per 10,000 as opposed to 1.22 for white U.K. born males – a fourteen-fold increase. McGovern and Cope's study (1987) found a similar pattern. For black men the rate was 13.8; for black women, 9.8 per 10,000 and for white men and women it was 2.05 and 0.7 respectively in the 16–29 years category.[74]

A number of reasons have been given to account for this striking racial difference. Racism, according to Littlewood, is so stressful to young black people that they eventually go mad.[75] Others, in particular Harris *et al*, argue strongly for the inclusion of genetic factors in the search for an answer to the pattern observed. They draw attention to conditions such as Down's Syndrome and neural tube defect which have a racial variation in rates and point out that there is no simple explanation for this variation and suggest that future investigations should cover a spectrum of possible factors. If this is true of these conditions, it must also be true of schizophrenia:

'Similarly, potential biological differences in terms of genetic factors, neuro-chemistry, pre- and peri-natal trauma, virology and immunology merit further investigation in relation to high rates of schizophrenia reported here, as well as attention to the possible effects of living in inner-city decaying areas with high unemployment and poor housing.'[76]

Others, however, are more explicit and more encompassing in their explanations. Rushworth locates madness among black people in a wider evolutionary framework. Reminiscent of the eugenicists discussed earlier, he links madness to low I.Q. and sexual promiscuity among black people. He believes that black people are genetically more likely to have a lower I.Q. than white people, that they are more likely to go mad, and are less sexually restrained, thus reproducing profusely like grass and frogs, and so surviving by sheer numbers.[77]

E

But for many black people these are spurious explanations which obfuscate rather than clarify the link between black people's experience and the high rates of admission into psychiatric institutions. Francis, Director of the Afro-Caribbean Mental Health Association, for example, dismisses Littlewood's assertion that racism makes black people go mad and argues that:

> 'If we want to use that hypothesis then a couple of centuries ago, during slavery, there should have been large scale mental disorder − the complete mental dissolution of black people − but on the contrary, there has been tremendous resilience, and people have been able to heal the wound.'[78]

It is, therefore, not the stress from the general racism which is at the heart of the over-representation of black people in mental hospitals but rather a specific type of racism which is operating in the process of assessment by the psychiatrists. Psychiatrists are not immune to the influence of racist stereotypes which portray black people as inherently aggressive, non-verbal and not able to think things through rationally. As it so happens, argues Francis, these stereotypes coincide with the first signs and symptoms of schizophrenia and this to a large extent influences the psychiatrist's assessment in the diagnosis.[79]

Sashidharan warns against putting too much emphasis on diagnosis as he sees this as only a small proportion of the problem. He points to the considerable involvement of other agencies in the process of bringing people into psychiatric hospitals. G.P.s, social workers, the police and the courts are all involved in the referral process. Psychiatrists are at the end of the long journey and Francis believes that if one is not mad at the beginning of that journey, 'by the time the various agencies are through with you, you may well be crazy'. Black people are not only over-represented in psychiatric hospitals but also in prisons, in special education units and in remand centres as well as in children's homes. What these institutions have in common, argues Sashidharan, is the coercive form of intervention in the lives of black people.[80]

## 3. Mental Illness in Liverpool

It was against the background of this debate that the field of mental illness among black people in Liverpool was approached. It was important to find out if the experience of black people in Liverpool was similar to that presented by the Bandung File report, and if so what could be done to meet the needs in this area. In order to establish the number of those in mental institutions, a decision was taken to conduct a small scale study for three months with one researcher collecting information on a day-to-day basis from psychiatric hospitals which serve the city. It was necessary to know the number of black people admitted; how long they were kept in hospital; whether they came in as informal patients or under section; how many of those sectioned applied for a Tribunal hearing; and what diagnosis was given after they were discharged.

To set up this study the permission of Psychiatric Consultants was required. As discussed earlier, consultants 'own' not only beds in their wards, but also patients. In approaching the Consultants through the Division of Psychiatry no problems were anticipated as it was believed that this would be a straightforward procedure where the researcher would go into the ward and identify any black patients admitted each day and obtain the rest of the information from the ward staff, who, for ethical reasons, would make sure that the researcher did not have access to the patients' names. Whilst the psychiatrists offered their full co-operation and support, they also insisted that a protocol should be produced describing in detail what was intended and that an application should be made to the Ethical Committee, a body which decides whether or not any research involving patients can be conducted. This demand was surprising as the Ethical Committee is more concerned with research involving the trial of drugs on patients rather than social research where there is no interference with the patient's body. This argument was not accepted and it was stated that unless these conditions were met, permission to conduct the research would not be granted.

To produce an effective application the help was enlisted of a very supportive geriatrician, who was familiar with such applications in the course of his own medical research. It was also a surprise to him that the Psychiatrists had made this demand for this kind of research. He suggested that the Chairman of the committee should be invited to discuss the draft application before submitting it formally. Four months after submission contact was made with the Chairman to find out what had happened and the researchers were informed that the committee was concerned with medical and not social research matters and that the application had been forwarded to the Unit Manager in one of the hospitals in which research was to be conducted. When this hospital was contacted the researcher was told there was no record of such an application. As the whole project had only two years to run it was thought inadvisable to start the whole process of application again. A decision was taken to do a headcount similar to the one carried out by members of the Black Social Workers Project in 1983. The Psychiatrists were still not keen on this alternative assessment but they dropped their objection at the meeting called by a non-medical Unit Manager in the psychiatric field who had been approached for support. It was decided to include in the statistics Day Care Centres, Hostels for both mentally ill and mentally handicapped, as well as Social Workers' case loads.

The figures collected showed that there had been very little change in the pattern since 1983. Unlike the national picture discussed in the Bandung File, Liverpool did not have an over-representation of black people in psychiatric institutions. Why? Asking this question does not imply in any way that it is desirable for black people to be over-represented. However, in terms of representation in the Liverpool population it is estimated that black people comprise between 7–10%. The headcount statistics showed that in psychiatric hospitals black people were 4.3% of the total, in psychiatric day hospitals 4.8%, in psychogeriatric hospitals 0.9% and in institutions for the mentally handicapped 2.6%.[81] These figures have been given weight by professionals – nurses, psychiatrists, community psychiatric nurses and social workers – who stated that they did not see many black patients in their respective areas of work. One Community Psychiatric nurse estimated that in the 11 years of her service in general psychiatry, she had probably seen only 20 black patients. In the last five years she has been working in the field of Psychotherapy and in that period has only treated two black patients. Her colleagues, our respondent informed us, report a similar situation. Does this mean that black people in Liverpool are less susceptible to factors leading to mental illness or mental handicap? Although this may be a comforting and indeed a reassuring suggestion about the resilience of black people, to assume automatically this to be the case is to ignore similar patterns of under-representation which the Area Profile Studies have shown to exist in Employment, Housing, Social Services, Education and Health. The emphasis in all these studies is on structural racism which has made these services and institutions inaccessible to black people. It is generally believed that the quality of treatment black people feel they would receive is crucial in determining the above figures, rather than the absence of these stresses.

The question that has been constantly asked by policy makers on this issue is what evidence exists to suggest that there are black people in the community who have these stresses and some forms of mental disorder. In other words how is it known that despite the above figures, black people like white people, do suffer from mental illness? This has not been idle questioning, but has been used as strong argument against requests to provide accessible and effective facilities for the black community in this area. The old tactics of 'prove to us through academic research with figures, that there are mentally ill black people out there' has been in full force in meetings where the question of provision for mentally ill black people has been raised. There are three main reasons why it was felt that this was not only an unrealistic demand but also that it was a diversionary tactic. One is that within the framework of action research, determining that there is a need does not depend on the prior collection of data in abstract, using conventional methodologies of social science research such as questionnaires in which people are asked 'are you suffering from mental illness?'. The low take-up reflected in the above figures and confirmed by professionals should be enough for a policy maker to say 'let us look at what we are doing and seek to provide this service differently in order to see if this will improve the effectiveness of the provision'. There are good examples of this approach in the Chinese Elderly People's Luncheon Club. Before specific provision was made for Chinese elderly people to use the Sheila Kay Day Centre on Wednesdays, there were hardly any Chinese people using Day Care facilities in Liverpool. Although at the beginning of the project only a few Chinese came to the Centre, at the time of this research over 40 were attending every Wednesday. What is different about Wednesdays in the Centre is that there are Chinese cooks, social workers, videos, library books and games. The elderly Chinese feel a sense of belonging, of security and freedom of communication with those running the centre on this day. They feel that their needs both physically and culturally are being met. The service is accessible to them and they avail themselves of that service. This is true of the Home Help Project and the Black Elders Luncheon Club. The need has always been there, but asking academic questions in abstract is not the most effective way of determining the extent of that need. Providing a service is a far more pragmatic and therefore realistic way of determining a need. Academic research, as it has been defined here, may have its place in the Social Science institutions but it certainly has no relevance in developing services for black people.

The second argument against questionnaire-style research was that it would not only be insulting to the people who were asked 'Are you mentally ill?' but it would also be dangerous for the researcher as such a question could possibly gain the interviewer a very well deserved 'smack on the face'. It really does not matter how well disguised the questions are. Given the attitude towards mental illness in this society people will feel, and know, they are still being asked 'Are you mad?' Many researchers have been thrown out of people's homes for asking less insulting questions than this. The final point relates to reliability. What measure does one use to detect psychiatric illness in another person? Let us assume that there are people who do not feel like punching the researchers on the face when asked whether or not they are mad and they respond by saying 'Oh no, I'm not mentally ill' or they say 'Oh yes, I'm quite mad'. What is the researcher to make of either answer? In this situation do people always respond to question-naires truthfully when it relates to what they feel or think? If they do, in the case of mental illness, how are they defining mental illness? From our previous discussion it is obvious that 'experts' do not agree on what is mental illness. Do individual people have their own measure of mental illness? And if they have, could a collection of individual definitions provide the means by which to draw conclu-sions about the extent of mental illness in the black community without asking people if they are 'mad'? One often quoted study is that conducted by Goldberg.[82]

Few would find faults in Goldberg's methodology in which he uses self-administered questionnaires in the detection of 'non-psychotic psychiatric illness' in the community. Many would agree that it meets the academic criteria of impersonality and universality in its applica-tion. But what even this kind of study cannot escape is the degree of restriction inherent in the questionnaire framework, the pre-conceptions of those who formulate the questions and interpret the findings, and more importantly, the way the results of the research can be used. Drawing from the work of C. Wright Mills, Staples has made this point more succinctly:

> 'Science in Sociology consists of the method. It is the responsibility of the Social Scientists to collect, organise and classify the data. But in their interpretation, the specific conclusions reached will be related to social goals and personal values and Sociologists are not inclined to reach conclusions from their research that tend to dim-inish the credibility of their own self-conceptions and institutional loyalties. Hence, while the method may be impersonal and univer-

sal, group membership and the values resulting therefrom are decisive in determining the use to which research will be put.[83]

As was pointed out above, black researchers are party to this process of biased interpretation as long as they operate within a traditional, academic, value-free framework.

For black people to know that all is not well in the area of mental health in the community does not require the implementation of prolonged 'scientific' studies. As far back as the early 1980's members of the Black Women's Group in Liverpool – now known as the Black Sisters – were confronted with the problem of many young people who had developed 'unusual behaviour' reflecting some form of mental disturbance. According to members of the Granby Community Mental Health Group (the activities of this group will be discussed later) the problem has increased. Many of them were born and still live in the community and they know many people with whom they attended school who are now exhibiting unusual behaviour or who have had 'mental breakdowns'. Discussion with people in the community reveals that there is a reluctance to enlist the help of existing health institutions for fear that the disturbed person may face racist practices including compulsory detention with a consequent deterioration in the physical and mental state of the person detained. In general, therefore, both relatives and the community have learned to cope and accommodate people with such behaviour and it is only when this process of containment breaks down, as a result of either the intensity of the condition or tensions within the family, that help will be sought from the institutions. There is no provision where black people feel they can find help without the danger of being incarcerated. Those who provide the statutory health service may indeed dismiss this allegation and argue that black people have no grounds for such fears. Whatever the argument the fact remains that this is the perception some black people have of the institutions, and that perception may be crucial in determining the take-up of psychiatric services and may indeed go a long way in explaining the under-representation reflected in the headcount exercise.

Three experiences, on which we shall report, provide grounds for the negative perceptions held. Two of these cases are of young black women who were admitted informally and found themselves detained under a Section Order. The other is of a middle aged black man whose story was told to us by his friends.

## 4. Case Studies

In the course of the project researchers became involved in a number of cases. One of these involved a young woman who will be called Jane. The researchers' involvement in this case came as a response to a cry for help from the community. This case study, which is reported on fully, is important for a number of reasons. Firstly, it was people in the community who asked for help. Secondly, it provides the opportunity to hear the patient tell her own story. Thirdly, the authenticity of her story was endorsed by her doctor who was interviewed during and after her stay in hospital. Finally, and perhaps most importantly, the observations the doctor made about the institution within which he worked raised serious questions about psychiatry in general and not simply in relation to black people. But before dealing with the case study it is important to discuss three sections of the 1983 Mental Health Act which were applied to Jane: Sections 5(2); 2 and 3.

Section 5(2) is used for the urgent detention of in-patients by the responsible medical officer or his/her deputy. The duration for this detention is 72 hours. If, after this period, it is deemed necessary for the patient to remain in hospital another Section is applied, one of which is Section 2. However, unlike Section 5(2) which needs only the signature of the responsible medical officer, Secton 2 is more complicated. It needs the recommendation of two doctors, one with 'special experience in the diagnosis and treatment of mental disorder' and one who has previous acquaintance with the patient.[84] A third recommendation must be made by an approved social worker. In urgent situations where a social worker is not immediately available the doctor may advise the nearest relative to be the third applicant for this Section to be applied. Section 2 is used to admit patients into hospital as well as to extend the period of detention of those already in hospital from 72 hours, (Section 5(2)) to 28 days. Section 2 cannot be extended. If it is necessary for the patient to remain in hospital after the 28 days, Section 3 is applied and its duration is for up to six months. If the patient wants to be discharged whilst still on Section 2 she/he must apply to the Mental Health Review Tribunal within the first 14 days of detention. If the relatives apply it must be 'within 28 days of the patient's discharge being barred by the RMO' (Responsible Medical Officer).[85] Whilst under Section patients may be granted leave of absence from hospital. Although some patients may be given leave without conditions attached, others may be asked to agree to come back to hospital at a specified time. Failure to meet this condition may involve informing the police who then have the responsibility to find and bring the patient back to hospital. This was a possibility facing Jane when we met her. She had been allowed three days leave of absence and was refusing to return to hospital. Not wanting the police to be involved researchers were asked to help persuade her to go back voluntarily. It was when she was taken back that the researchers met the doctor who was later interviewed.

### a. Jane's Experience

Jane was a young black woman in her twenties whose 'unusual behaviour' started after she had her first baby. In common parlance this is 'post-natal blues'. Behaviour on occasions became so intense that she ended up in hospital. It was not possible to find out from Jane whether or not she had been sectioned on those occasions or whether she came in as an informal patient. But on the occasion the researchers met her she had gone in as an informal patient. She had had an argument with her partner late at night and she went into hospital to find refuge. The doctor who saw her that Friday night (the same doctor who was looking after her and whom the researchers were able to interview) told how very distressed Jane was when she came in; she stated that she did not want any treatment but just a bed and sleeping tablets. She was allowed to stay over the weekend as an informal patient.

According to the doctor interviewed, who will be called Dr. Jones, the problem started on Monday morning when the Senior Registrar met Jane. At this interview Jane talked at length about what she saw as major world problems and insisted that staff must be made aware of these major issues. She refused to leave the interview room arguing that for staff to understand these problems they would need her help. What were these major problems? Dr. Jones was asked:

> 'She tended to want to discuss major political issues, major social issues particularly issues relating to race.'

At this interview the Registrar became irritated and prescribed a small dose of a major tranquillizer. At this stage Jane had not been diagnosed and the researchers had difficulty understanding how the Registrar reached a decision as to which of the many drugs to prescribe. Dr. Jones gave clarification. There are three kinds of supposedly treatable mental illnesses, depression, schizophrenia and mania. Initially, treatment is given on the basis of a provisional diagnosis which presumably can be changed in the light of new evidence pointing to another diagnosis. In the case of schizophrenia and mania a change in diagnosis from one to the other does not really matter because both conditions are treated by the same major tranquillizers. It seems quite disturbing that someone who has been admitted informally and whose main form of 'unusual behaviour' is talking at length on 'major issues' should have a major tranquillizer prescribed for her.

In the afternoon on the same day Jane insisted on joining another Consultant's round and continued her morning talk on world issues. She was asked to leave and according to Dr. Jones who was part of the team, she was extremely reluctant to do so:

> 'It was quite heartbreaking to watch in that you saw a number of skilled psychotherapists who were in the room applying their ability acquired over a period of years to persuade people to do things without being in anyway unpleasant and failing totally. First the Consultant, then the Registrar, then the Social Worker, and also myself, although I wouldn't put myself in that category, I mean I don't have the same expertise. And there she was, sitting in the chair. Eventually confronted by a large number of nurses who were obviously prepared to carry her out, she went saying, not unreasonably, "I don't want any violence!".'

The following afternoon Jane's own Consultant was doing his 'rounds' with his team when she engaged the team in her discussion of world problems. The Consultant was told that Jane was refusing to take the prescribed major tranquillizer. On this occasion she refused to leave the interview room. But the Consultant filled in the form for Section 5(2) applying a 72 hour compulsory detention during which Jane could be forced to take the prescribed drugs which were deemed to be clinically necessary. At the same time the Consultant, who will be called Dr. James, set in motion the process of further form filling in preparation for Section 2. We asked Dr. Jones if, in his view, Jane's behaviour merited the prescription of a major tranquillizer and a Section:

> 'I don't wish to stick my neck out and I also have great respect for Dr James. He has also written a good reference for my next job, so I must not be too unkind to the man and do him a great disservice. But I feel in all fairness and in simple human terms it is understandable that at the time he was annoyed and that may have made his decision more precipitate. I think, however good your system of

mental health may be, there will be a human element, there will be a
degree to which because someone is angry, they will get on with the
thing quicker. I would hope when something is appropriate it could
not be said that because Dr James was angry the Section was
applied but that it would not have been applied if he was not angry.
But I think on that day he was probably a little bit angry.'

Dr. Jones was sure that had he been making the decisions he would
not have sectioned Jane. He would have waited for at least two days
and tried to persuade her to take her medication and to get staff to
work with her to make her realise that it was in her own interest to
take the prescribed drugs. For Dr. Jones a Section should normally be
for people who are a threat to themselves or to others and Jane was
not in that category. What she needed was space and time to sort
herself out, space to be allowed to behave in an odd and slightly
disturbed way perhaps, without applying drugs to curb that
behaviour. Only when the situation gets worse i.e. when she does not
eat, drink or sleep can physical intervention be justified. Dr. Jones,
however, was aware that this form of response to 'slightly disturbed
behaviour' in the hospital where Jane was detained was not possible
to achieve:

'The problem in the hospital where I work is very much one of
inadequate staffing; that tragically there is much less talking going
on and much giving out of pills, locking up doors and dishing out
dinners. I think in many ways there is a parallel with the complaints
of the prison service where prison officers say what they do is
locking and unlocking doors, and have no time to talk to prisoners. I
hate to use the analogy of prison and mental hospitals, but it is true
that in the hospital in which I work a small number of people do get
detained against their will and the thing most similar to that is a
prison. I can't think of anything that is similar to it.'

There is, of course, a school of thought which supports the use of
drugs in the treatment of 'mental illness'. The belief here, in line with
the psychiatric perspective discussed earlier, is that in 'mental illness'
the brain substance is diseased and 'normality' can be restored by
drug therapy. Dr. Jones was not in agreement with this view and felt
that, in general, major tranquillizers modified behaviour rather than
cured the underlying cause of the 'disturbed behaviour'.

In the course of her stay in hospital and whilst under medication
Jane's perceived 'unusual behaviour' increased rather than decreased.

She told Dr. Jones that she believed she was a potential African Queen but refused to tell him why she thought so, arguing that since Dr. Jones never discussed his own personal matters with her, why should she discuss hers with him. Dr. Jones admitted that for him Jane's assertion of being a potential African Queen was so unlikely that he felt it might have been a delusion in psychiatric terms and he used a political analogy to make his point:

> 'It is possible for Derek Hatton to believe, despite all his political problems, that he will be the Prime Minister in the future. One can see the mechanism from being a City Councillor to being a Prime Minister, but although not impossible, it is more unlikely for a Liverpool 8 housewife who is not involved in politics to become a future Prime Minister.'

Yet in Jane's case her claim to African royalty is not as unfounded and irrational as it appeared to Dr. Jones and his colleagues. When this was discussed with Jane she described how her father was of African Royal descent and she believed that if her family went back to Africa she would be Queen. But the staff in hospital, including Dr. Jones, did not know this link, hence the tendency to see this as a sign of delusion. This is crucial because it raises again the question of what in fact people define as 'mental illness'. Using the above situation it is certainly not what people say that is important but whether or not what they say appears rational to those putting people in categories of 'sane' or 'insane'. But is it really justified to section people and put them under major tranquillizers just because what they say and do is irrational? Is this what psychiatry as a rational science is supposed to be about? This question was put to Dr. Jones:

> 'If you look at it philosophically the only thing anyone is really sure about is one's own consciousness. That being the case the whole situation becomes horrendously difficult. One of the reasons I feel disillusionment in my job is that I find it very difficult to apply now, or to say that I am applying, the simple rule of thumb that I was taught to apply in psychiatry as a student. In that rule I felt that I cannot say whether somebody else's reality, somebody else's feelings that they are the Prime Minister, the Queen of Africa or whatever, or that space ships land in their living room, or whatever else they say, is not true. There may indeed be spaceships landing in their living rooms. I just can't see them. The rule of thumb I applied as a student was that if that reality was unpleasant for them, then I would

seek to change it. But in the job I am in at present, you can't use that rule of thumb. You are not allowed to. You are expected to treat someone from the point of view of their future mental health and potential consequences. So I am now extending the concept of unpleasant from an actual unpleasant reality that they don't want spaceships landing in their living rooms to an anxiety about potential consequences that if someone believes there are spaceships landing in the living room they may also start to believe that they can fly and in consequence may jump off tall buildings. This is a hypothesis and it cannot be assumed that all patients will go through this sequence. That is why I feel so disillusioned in what I am doing at the moment.'

During one of the researchers' visits to see Jane there was some discussion with another black woman, who was a patient in Jane's ward. Her view was that the hospital was racist and that all black people were treated as criminals in the wards, 'we are all under Section here'. This subject was raised with Dr. Jones. Did he think racism was implicated in the way black people were treated in the hospital?

'I have been thinking about this one, it is quite interesting. Although it is a small sample of people, I have been in this job over 9 months now and I think I have only treated 7 black people (4 women, 3 men), of those 5 were Sectioned. The other thing interesting is that of the 5, four were women. The sample is too small to be significant statistically, but it is nevertheless interesting. It can certainly be construed as being racist. But I don't believe the hospital is deliberately racist.'

Dr. Jones' assertion that racism could not be the main reason for the pattern he observed was based on the multi-racial composition of staff in this hospital – doctors and nurse employees. As he described it, the hospital has a 'cosmopolitan staff'. He was more inclined to believe that social factors and not 'race' were responsible for the experience of black people in psychiatric hospitals:

'People from Liverpool 8 and similar areas may well express themselves in more overt, at least verbally aggressive and sometimes physically aggressive ways so that their desire to leave would tend to be met with a Section whereas people from a middle class, professional background may express themselves in a way that can be more easily reasoned with and perhaps can be more easily persuaded to stay and therefore, are less likely to be detained through a Section. I think you would find that people from Liverpool 8 both black and white tend to be sectioned a lot compared to those from middle class areas.'

Whilst few would disagree with Dr Jones' observation, it is interesting to note that he later discussed the case of a white working class man in the same hospital who believed that he was the nephew of Queen Victoria. This patient was, however, not under Section even though his alleged link to the Royal Family was less plausible than Jane's. When this was put to him, he accepted that black people do have additional problems:

'I feel that there are all sorts of problems particularly relating to Jane that have a lot to do with the black community, resulting in them in one way or another getting a bad deal. I think the first one is a situation of tension in Toxteth that leads people to distrust anything that has to do with white establishments. When black patients, like the one you spoke to, say the hospital is racist, they are saying it as part of a learned response which was learned outside the hospital. It is very difficult for a black person from that background, particularly when under stress, to accept any form of help from any white establishment. That is one problem. The other is the whole question of police involvement in that community. If a patient who is under Section absconds from hospital or in the case of Jane, does not come back per arrangement, we are bound by law to inform the police if we feel that the patient may be a risk to herself or the community. This is really to cover ourselves.'

But Dr. Jones felt that because of the sensitive relationship between the police and the black community, the police might be reluctant to send a car to the area. If they do the person may be mistakenly perceived by the community as a criminal or a collaborator with the police. The link between mental health/psychiatry and the police leads to the re-enforcement of the negative views already held about psychiatry and its role in the lives of black people.

For Dr. Jones the use of police in getting patients back into hospital is unacceptable. Patients, he believed, should be persuaded and not coerced to come back. There ought to be a facility to send nurses and not the police to talk to them. As far as he knew there was one community psychiatric nurse on call for 24 hours and no suggestion had been made to use this nurse to bring back absconded patients.

Under the 1983 Mental Health Act the powers and rights of patients are supposed to be safeguarded by the right of appeal to the Mental Health Review Tribunal within a specified period. In accordance with this legal provision all patients under Section are issued with a leaflet in hospital informing them of their rights and how to appeal to the Tribunal and also how to obtain legal aid. If these pieces of paper were given to patients by people who do not believe that the patients are 'mentally ill', it would perhaps make sense. The irony is that the same people who have decided that the patient has a diminished mental capacity expect them to understand and act on the information contained in these leaflets. Many patients like Jane, who had been issued with this legal advice, had not even looked at the paper. Dr. Jones says:

> 'Jane's leaflet on legal aid was handed to me by another patient after Jane absconded. It was still in its envelope. She hadn't looked at it as far as I could see, so that one wonders about the ability of a sectioned patient who is certainly distressed and probably ill at the time, to organise themselves well enough to get together with a solicitor and to find out how they can get legal aid – unless they are that sort of person who does that kind of thing anyway. For most patients . . . who came from not educated backgrounds it is difficult even to submit the appeal.'

The leaflet given to sectioned patients was examined. One does not have to be mentally disturbed to fail to understand what the jargon is all about. The message is so obscure that it frightens rather than empowers people. Some of those who read the information pick up odd words like 'solicitor' or 'legal aid' and become convinced that more disaster is to befall them. The printing is so small that if a person has poor eyesight they would have no chance to decipher the wording. One team is so conscious of the inadequacy of this document that they have made it policy to apply for a Tribunal on behalf of every elderly patient sectioned and is now mounting a campaign with the help of Mental Health Commission to produce a more sensible and easy to understand leaflet on Patients' Rights when Sectioned. It is the duty of the hospital to ensure that the patient and their relatives understand fully the message in the leaflet. Nurses do read out the rights, but how can anyone absorb this at the same time as being told they have lost their freedom? The information on these leaflets must also be given to relatives.

There are, of course, people who are quite competent in understanding their rights and indeed many have taken their cases to the Tribunal. Had Jane taken her case to the Tribunal what would have been her chances of winning? Dr. Jones responded:

'The appeal is being heard essentially by people who think in the same kind of way as the psychiatrist, the other doctor and the social worker who originally filled in forms for the Section in the first place. Now this leads us to the greyest area of all which is what is mental illness. I think most people would agree on the definition in cases of the more bizarre forms of disturbed behaviour. But Jane particularly highlights the case of somebody who is very much against estab- lished authority. I think if that is all they are, the answer is they are not mentally ill. But I mean the fight against established authority can be used, and it certainly has been used in the Soviet Union and I don't believe that, as it is often construed, all psychiatric doctors in the Soviet Union misapply their understanding of mental illness and deliberately detain people who they feel are not really ill. It is just that they feel that dissidents, people who question authority, must be mentally ill because they are questioning authority.'

No doubt those who sit on Mental Health Review Tribunals will take issue with Dr. Jones on his assessment of the functioning of the Tribunal and the values that guide their decision making. They will argue rightly that many patients who have taken their cases to the Tribunal have been successful. The point is, however, about the use of psychiatry on those who question established authority in whatever setting and the consensus about that use in the wider society. Jane was sectioned because on one occasion she refused to leave the room when asked to do so by the medical officer who has an established authority as a psychiatrist. She insisted on talking about racism and wanted staff to recognise this as a serious issue in the world. Had she gone to the Tribunal and insisted at the hearing to sit in on the private session and discuss racism, what would have happened then? Had she challenged the established authority of the Mental Health Review Tribunal as vigorously as she challenged the hospital staff would she have won her case? Some black people who have been in similar situations will be able to answer this question but in Jane's case the answer will never be known because she did not take her case to the Tribunal. As she said, she was not going to bother with any of these racist white institutions as they are all the same, and she settled down to a routine of drug therapy.

Three months after the first meeting with Jane the friend who asked the researchers to help her to go back to hospital, rang to say that Jane was really not well and had developed uncontrollable shaking movements. She was out of hospital on drug therapy which included an injection once a fortnight. A second interview was held with Dr. Jones who was still looking after her. He said that Jane was on a major tranquillizer called Fluphrenazine. She was also on Haloperidol three times a day and on a sleeping tablet called Phionidazine. According to Dr. Jones any of these drugs could cause shaking because they all have Parkinsonian side effects. However, Dr. Jones believed that it could be the Fluphrenazine injection which was responsible because it was given in a large dose to cover the patient for two weeks. Dr. Jones explained that it was necessary to give the drug in an injection form because Jane did not want to take tablets. However, to counteract the side effects she had to take Procyclidine tablets! It was pointed out to Dr. Jones that if Jane was not keen on taking tablets was it not unlikely that she would take Procyclidine? He admitted that it was a difficulty about which he was concerned. Such major tranquillizers when taken over a long period – five to ten years, could actually damage the brain and the patient could be left with permanent Parkinsonian side effects, stated Dr. Jones. Jane is still on major tranquillizers and her condition has deteriorated so much that it supports Francis's observation that if you are not mad at the beginning, 'by the time the various agencies are through with you, you may well be crazy'.

*b. Janet's story*

The phone rang at about 3.30 p.m. and it was Sue, the woman who had asked us to persuade Jane (see previous case study) to go back to hospital. Sue was concerned, another young black woman, whom we shall call Janet, had been sectioned. Janet's father was out of town and her 24 year old sister, whom we shall call Pam, was trying to deal with the situation. Sue had been told that the Consultant was going to be at the hospital at 4 p.m. and she wanted me to be there as well so that we could both meet the Consultant and find out why Janet had been sectioned.

I arrived at the hospital before Sue and asked the staff if I could see Janet but this was refused since it was not visiting time. Sue soon arrived, and on the strength of her being a friend of the family, we were reluctantly allowed into Janet's room. The staff seemed uncomfortable about our presence and one said 'You have come to try and get her out of here haven't you?'

There were already two visitors with Janet, one of whom was her sister, Pam. We asked Janet to tell us about the events that led to her admission. She then related what she described as the worst night-mare in her life.

Janet lived in a flat with her favourite pets, a dog and a cat. She had not been sleeping well recently because of various problems in her life and when her dog was injured in an attack she became so upset she decided to take some sleeping tablets so that she could have a long sleep and a rest. She took the tablets on Sunday night and did not wake up until Monday evening. When she woke up she panicked, having realised how long she had slept. She phoned her friend, asking her to go with her to hospital. When they arrived at hospital A, Janet was told that she would be admitted but was first allowed to go home to get her nightdress. She returned within half an hour and spent the night still in a dazed state.

On Tuesday she was transferred to an acute psychiatric ward in hospital B. She was still very tired when she arrived and asked to be allowed to sleep.

> 'They took me to a bed in a ward that was empty at the time. I fell asleep immediately and when I woke up the lights were on and there were all these people around. Some of them were curled up in chairs and others were looking vacantly into space. Someone collapsed on the floor and nobody bothered to pick her up, they just walked past her. I was very frightened, I just thought if I stay here I will end up like them so I just ran out to the corridor to find a phone and told Pam to come and get me out of here.'

When Pam had phoned hospital B on Tuesday afternoon to find out if she could see Janet she had been told that she should come at evening visiting time. Pam arrived with 'get well cards' but was told she could not see Janet because she was asleep. She was reassured that Janet was comfortable and she need not worry. She left, asking the staff to put the cards on Janet's bedside locker so that when she woke up she would know she had been to see her. Pam was therefore surprised when she later received a frantic phone call from Janet on Tuesday night:

> 'She was very upset and was crying. She said "can you please get me out of here". I told her I thought she was alright. She said "what do you mean, have you been here? You don't know what this place is like". I told her I had been and I left her some cards with the staff. She told me nobody had given her any cards and they were not on

the locker and she wanted to come home. I told Janet to put the phone down and that I would phone her back after I had spoken to the staff in her ward.'

When Pam rang the hospital she was told that Janet was comfortable and was still asleep. She told them that this was not the case and asked if Janet could sign herself out. The staff told her this was not advisable because it would not be good for Janet's health if she went home, besides she did not want to sign herself out. They told Pam that Janet was not being kept against her will. Pam then said she intended to take Janet home, but the staff told her that they would have to call the doctor to Janet. The hospital said they would ring Pam when the doctor had been. Pam said she waited for an hour before the phone rang and it was Janet:

'She was hysterical. The doctor had been and told her that she was now sectioned and could not come home.'

Pam then rang the hospital to plead with the staff to let Janet come home. She even promised to bring her into hospital every day to see the doctor if that was felt necessary but she was told the Section could not be lifted.

Janet refused to stay in the main ward and insisted on sleeping in a separate room. She explained that she would have been frightened to fall asleep with all the people whom she saw as 'strange'. The staff gave her some tablets which she refused to take but they insisted and waited until they were sure she had swallowed them.

We asked Janet what happened when the doctor came to see her on Tuesday night:

'When she came I was still very upset. She asked why I had wanted to kill myself. I told her I did not want to kill myself, I just wanted a long sleep. She then asked if I would do it again. I told her no, and she wanted to know what I wanted to do. I told her I wanted to go home. I told her I was worried about my injured dog and my cat. I wanted to go and look after them. I told her I would come to the hospital to see her every day for whatever treatment she thought necessary. I really thought this doctor understood what I was saying but then she said "You are not going anywhere, you are going to stay here for 72 hours and then we will review the situation. If we think it necessary we will keep you here for six months." The thought of staying in this place for six months!'

Janet became very upset again but we reassured her that it might not come to that. The Consultant was two hours late but Sue and I were prepared to wait until he came so we could discuss the possibility of lifting the Section. Janet then brought up another worrying aspect of her stay in hospital, this was about the meals. The staff asked her if there was any food she did not like to eat. She told them she ate most things but did not eat any vegetables. Pam confirmed that even as a child Janet did not like vegetables:

> 'But when my meal came, all I could see was just a heap of vegetables. There probably was some other food underneath but I was put off and told them I did not want to eat. They then said "that's one meal you have refused to eat".'

The following morning Janet was late for her breakfast and when she asked for toast, she was told that the ovens had been cleaned and could not be used again:

> 'I thought I would eat some cornflakes but they were so soggy. I think someone must have spilt milk in them. They were really disgusting so I did not finish them. They then said "that is another meal you have not eaten". I just felt as if they were making a big issue about the whole thing.'

This was more worrying than Janet realised because refusing to eat or drink can be a symptom of depressive illness and is one of the criteria used to determine whether or not a patient is a danger to themselves. It therefore provides justification for a Section. If the staff were interpreting these incidents as refusals to eat rather than a rejection of unacceptable meals the chances of Janet's release from a section would be diminished.

Whilst we were in Janet's room, taking notes, a member of staff came to ask if Janet wanted a cup of tea. Soon after another member of staff came to say that the long awaited Consultant had come and was ready to see Janet. Within a few minutes the Consultant sent for Pam. Both came back to inform us that Janet was discharged and that the hospital would arrange a follow-up visit at home. The two young women then asked what it meant to be sectioned. When we explained that the Act is used on people who are believed to be mentally ill, Janet's eyes filled with tears and she said quietly, as if talking to herself:

> 'But why do they think I am mentally ill? Why do they want to make out that I am mad?'

Sue put her arms around her and reassured her that she was alright, and not mentally ill.

Janet's experience presents as disturbing and depressing a picture of the hospital psychiatric service as that painted by Van Gogh in his 'Cornfield with crows' three days before he committed suicide. It also raises a number of questions:

1. Why did an 18 year old woman with no previous history of mental illness, who went into hospital voluntarily, end up in an acute psychiatric ward?
2. On Monday night after arriving in hospital A, Janet was allowed to go home to get her nightdress. Her prompt return surely reflected an adult rational response of someone who was concerned about her own well being. At some stage a decision was taken to transfer Janet to another hospital. A transfer from one hospital to another is a daunting enough experience for any patient, and it needs careful explanation to allay fears but this is even more so when the transfer is into a psychiatric ward. This was not done sufficiently enough in Janet's case. Why?
3. An admission into a psychiatric ward implies that a diagnosis of mental illness had already been made but before such a diagnosis can be made there should be a discussion and consultation with the patient and, if possible, with relatives as well before admission. This certainly would be considered good practice. Janet informed us that nobody had asked her about her problems. She was adamant that she had no intention of killing herself, she was desperate to have a sleep and that is why she took the tablets. No discussion occurred with her relatives. On the basis of the information to hand, what indication was there to suggest that an admission to an acute psychiatric ward was necessary?
4. Let us assume that the action taken by hospital A was based on the belief that Janet had deliberately taken an overdose. This brings us to the procedure followed when patients with overdose come to hospital A. Who decides what happens to such patients? Presumably if the overdose causes anxiety for the patient's physical health, a medical admission will be necessary. If there are no fears of physical damage from the overdose and the duty doctor decides the mental state is reasonable, is the patient discharged immediately without the offer of any follow-up? At what stage, using what guidelines is a patient considered sufficiently disturbed to be referred for a psychiatric opinion? Who decides whether or not only

social work support is necessary? These are crucial questions the answers to which imply the existence of a clear policy with a well spelt out code of practice. Is there such a policy? If there is, its application in practice should be known not only to the health workers but also to patients and the population at large since we are all potential patients.

5. The problem for Janet started on Tuesday night when she woke up and realised that she was in a psychiatric ward. She became upset, frightened and frantic. This is when she wanted to go home, to run away from what she saw as a nightmare. But can that upset behaviour under those circumstances be considered so unreasonable as to merit a Section? Who would not be upset under the same situation?

6. Section 5(2) lasts for 72 hours. Janet was not only released from this Section after 50 hours but she was also discharged from hospital. How rigorous was the assessment on the basis of which the Section was recommended if 50 hours later a person is deemed well enough to be discharged? Everyone, including medical personnel, can make a mistake. Could a mistake have been made in the assessment process? If that is the case, could that mistake be rectified by removing the Section from Janet's medical records?

To have a mental illness record can have devastating consequences to the social, economic and psychological life of an individual. Many employers are reluctant to employ people with such records. The existence of such a record can tip the balance against the holder when decisions are made about taking children into care or, in the case of divorce, which parent should have custody of the children. Even though the first Section was a mistake, it nevertheless serves as a point of reference in making assessment on the mental state of the individual in subsequent interactions with the health service, social workers, the courts etc.

Despite claims of enlightened attitudes, mental illness is still perceived as a discreditable attribute and many people who are so labelled still feel a sense of shame and, therefore, try to hide the fact that they have been sectioned. One of the ways to achieve this, Goffman suggests, is by passing. Passing is an attempt by stigma bearers to conceal the discredited condition and thus, pass for 'normal'. But this demands a constant editing of information given to others and a 'management of tension' when one has to make decisions 'to tell or not to tell; to let on or not to let on; to lie or not to lie; and in each case, to whom, how, when and where'.[86] The whole process, as Morgan *et al* states 'involves a high psychological cost'.[87] The cost, it could be argued, remains the same whether or not the Section was justified. People who have been sectioned will have to hide this fact if they want to emigrate to certain countries. America, Canada and Australia, for example, will not accept people with a history of mental illness. If it is accepted that mistakes can be made in taking decisions to section people, then something must be done to ensure that such mistakes are rectified. Our enquiries have revealed that there is no such clause in the 1983 Mental Health Act. This is a serious flaw in the Act which needs urgent attention by the Government, the Commissioners, the legal system as well as those responsible for Medical Health Tribunals.

7. On discharge, Janet was told that a follow-up visit would be arranged. Six weeks after discharge no one had called and no letter had been received, asking her to attend any clinic or day centre. Does this indicate that the hospital had no real fears about Janet's mental state, which in turn suggests that she should not have been sectioned, or is it a question of poor service delivery?

### c. John's story

John's experience was told by three independent informants: his friends, who were with him just before he fell ill; his relative who came to see him after he was told about John's condition, and people in the hospital where John was admitted. John was a 51 year old man who lived on his own. He was a respected member of the community and was an Elder in his church. On this particular day, he went to church at 5 a.m. to conduct a service. When he returned home at 6 a.m. he collapsed and could not move his legs which had become extremely painful. He crawled to the phone to ask for help from his friends:

> 'When we got there, he was still on the floor. He had pains in his legs. We were very alarmed by his condition, so we called an ambulance and some of us went with him to hospital.'

John was taken to hospital A where he was examined. The doctor told his friends that he could not find anything wrong with him and asked them to take him home. But by 2 p.m. his condition had worsened. He had convulsive attacks and had developed an unquenchable thirst. His friends called the ambulance and for the second time John was taken to hospital.

A number of tests were carried out including a chest X-ray. According to the relative the doctor remarked that the results of the X-ray showed that John's heart had grown bigger than in the previous test. Another doctor who was described as a 'psychologist' to the relatives, came and examined John. He used pins on his legs to detect if he had any feelings in them.

> 'They asked him to walk around the room, but he could not do so on his own, he held on to me.'

Again the doctor suggested that John was taken home as they could not find anything wrong with him. The relative explained that he lived on his own and asked if the hospital could keep him for observation. They were told that there were no beds available.

> 'I begged the doctor to keep him and asked him to find the bed anywhere as long as there will be nurses and doctors to look after him. So I was quite relieved when the doctor found a bed for him.'

John eventually arrived at hospital B just after 8.00 p.m. He was taken into an acute psychiatric ward. By 9 p.m. he was still sitting in the wheelchair waiting to be seen by a doctor. He was clutching his chest with pain and was still asking for water to drink. At 9.45, still sitting in the wheelchair, he collapsed and died.

These three case studies serve to demonstrate some of the complex issues which confront the black community in the area of mental health. Whilst only three accounts of hospital experience have been cited, many others have recounted similar stories of problems and difficulties in their dealings with mental health services. Although these studies have focussed attention on the way in which black people are dealt with, they present matters of concern for all. They raise important and serious questions of policy and practice at a number of levels: the professional, the political and the legal.

At a professional level there is an urgent need for psychiatry as a discipline to open the doors to critical evaluation of the ways in which mental illness is defined and diagnosed. It is important for practitioners in this field to be constantly aware that they are not involved in an area of pure 'scientific objectivity'. The definition and diagnosis of mental illness is contextual and is very much influenced by cultural, class, gender and racial issues. The example quoted earlier of Edna Higginbottom, who was committed to an asylum for 20 years for having pre-marital sex, attests to this. If psychiatry has been used in the past as a form of social control, it is possible that it can be used in that way now. That in fact is a view held by some black people who believe that psychiatry is used as a 'disposal option' by the courts in an attempt to control rebellion by black people. It is therefore crucial that practitioners engage in positive, supportive, non-conflictual discussions with people drawn from other disciplines and the general public in order to arrive at an understanding of what is involved in mental illness in terms of definitions, causes and diagnosis. It is only through such understanding that appropriate treatment can be established.

Mental illness is not just a medical but also a political issue. The diagnosis, admission and treatment procedures are carried out within the guidelines of the 1983 Mental Health Act. The major concern here is that within the Act there is no provision which enables the practitioners to erase a 'Section' record from a patient's medical history notes even if, with hindsight, it is realised that putting a patient under 'Section' was a mistake. Even when a patient takes the case to the Tribunal and the decision is that the 'Section' was unfairly applied, the record is still not removed from the patient's notes, despite the fact that such a record, as stated earlier, has horrendous social and economic implications for the individual.

All patients who have been put under 'Section' have a right to legal aid. One of the reasons behind this aspect of the Mental Health Act is to safeguard the rights of patients against the excesses of power by practitioners in their application of the Section. The information on this procedure, contained in a leaflet, is read out to the patient, who is then given the leaflet to keep. Although the aims here are good, in reality the procedure followed to achieve them is not very effective. Some patients may be too upset by the 'sectioning' to understand fully what is read out to them. Others may be too confused by the information itself, and others may be too disturbed. The leaflet itself is not written in a way which can be easily understood by all. The print is small and the language tends to be technical. It is important therefore to evaluate this practice if its objectives are to be met. Patients as well as relatives should have the information read and explained to them as an ongoing process, rather than as a one-off event at the time of sectioning. The leaflet needs re-writing and restructuring in a way that makes it easier to read and follow its message.

It is vitally important that all these issues are addressed urgently in order to ensure that the mental health service is not only freely available and accessible, but that it is also accountable and deals sensitively and appropriately with all sections of the community, both black and white, male and female.

The information presented in these six Consultative Papers highlights the problems faced by black people in the field of health. But this is only the tip of an iceberg. More work needs to be done if the totality of the problem is to be exposed. Without this total exposition, it is impossible to engage in a meaningful policy formulation and implementation which would ensure better health for all communities.

Before we conclude and offer recommendations, we wish to discuss two successful community initiatives in which the researchers in this Project were involved. These two initiatives – the Translation and Interpreting Service, and the Granby Community Health Drop-In Centre (Mary Seacole House) – demonstrate the difficult path black community groups have to tread when they attempt to establish services needed by their communities. On the positive side, they are the first moves in the attempt to begin to tackle some of the problems raised in the Consultative Papers.

## References

1. Spitzer, R. L., 'More on pseudoscience in science and the case for psychiatric diagnoses', *Archives of General Psychiatry*, 33, 1976, pp. 459–470.
2. Wing, J., *Reasoning About Madness*, London: Oxford University Press, 1978.
3. Szasz, T., *The Myth of Mental Illness*, Secker and Warburg, 1962.
4. Szasz, T., *Law, Liberty and Psychiatry*, Routledge and Kegan Paul, 1974, p. 14.
5. Scheff, T. J., *Being Mentally Ill: a Sociological Theory*, Aldine, 1966.
6. Szasz, T., *op cit*, 1962.
7. Szasz, T., *op cit*, 1974, p. 11.
8. Ibid, p.17.
9. *The Guardian*, 17 October 1989.
10. Ibid.
11. Ibid.
12. Szasz, T., *op cit*, 1974, p. x.
13. Ibid.
14. Ibid, p. xiii.
15. Scheff, T. J., *op cit*.
16. Horwitz, A. U., *The Social Control of Mental Illness*, Academic Press, 1982.
17. Goffman, E., *Asylums*, Harmondsworth, Penguin, 1969.
18. Stanton, A. H. and Schwartz, M. S., *The Mental Hospital*, New York, Basic Books, 1954.

19. Hollingshead, A. B. and Redlich, F. C., *Social Class and Mental Illness*, John Wiley and Sons Inc., 1958.

20. Horwitz, A. U., *op cit*, p. 2.

21. Ibid, p. 4.

22. Ibid, p. 14.

23. Benedict, R., 'Anthropology and the Abnormal', *Journal of General Psychology*, 10, 1934, pp. 59–80.

24. Hollingshead, A. B. and Redlich, F. C., *op cit*.

25. Magaro, P., 'Culture of Madness and its Treatment' in Magaro, P., (ed.), *The Construction of Madness*, Pergamon, 1976.

26. Ibid, p. 53.

27. Ibid, p. 56.

28. Littlewood, R. and Lipsedge, M., *Aliens and Alienists*, Penguin Books, 1982, p. 47.

29. Haley, A., *Roots*, Picador, 1978.

30. Carruthers, J. C., *Psychiatry of the Mau Mau*, Nairobi, 1954.

31. Gordon, E. B., 'Mentally Ill West Indian Immigrants', *British Journal of Psychiatry*, Vol. III, 1965, pp. 877–887.

32. Murphy, H. B. M., *Flight and Settlement*, UNESCO, Paris and Geneva, 1955.

33. Maizberg, B. *et al*, *Migration and Mental Disorder*, New York, 1956.

34. Kiev, A., 'Psychiatric Morbidity of West Indian Immigrants in an Urban Group Practice', *British Journal of Psychiatry*, Vol. III, 1956, pp. 51–56.

35. Hemsi, L. K. P., 'Psychiatric Morbidity of West Immigrants', *Social Psychiatry*, No. 2, 1967.

36. Mashmi, F., 'Community Psychiatric Problems Among Birmingham Immigrants', *Journal of Social Psychiatry*, No. 2, 1968.

37. Burke, Aggrey W., 'Attempted Suicide Among Asian Immigrants in Birmingham', *British Journal of Psychiatry*, Vol. 128, 1976, pp. 528–533.

38. Schofield, J., 'Behind the Veil: The Mental Health of Asian Women in Britain', *Health Visitor*, Vol. 54.5, 1981, pp. 183–186.

39. Hitch, P. J. and Rack, P. H., 'Mental Illness Among Polish and Russian Refugees in Bradford', *British Journal of Psychiatry*, Vol. 137, 1980, pp. 206–211.

40. Cochrane, R., 'Psychological and Behavioural Disturbances in West Indians, Indians and Pakistanis in Britain, a Comparison of Rates among Children and Adults', *British Journal of Psychology*, Vol. 134, 1979, pp. 201–210.

41. Brewin, C., 'Explaining the Lower Rates of Psychiatric Treatment among Asian Immigrants to the United Kingdom: a Preliminary Study', *Social Psychiatry*, Vol. 15, 1980, pp. 17–19.

42. Bebbington, P. E. *et al*, 'Psychiatric Disorders in Selected Immigrant Groups in Camberwell', *Social Psychiatry*, Vol. 16, 1981, pp. 43–51.

43. Brent Community Health Council, *op cit*, 1981.

44. Kiev, A., 'Beliefs and Delusions of West Indian Immigrants', *British Journal of Psychiatry*, Vol. 109, 1963, pp. 356–363.

45. Copeland, J. R. M., 'Aspects of Mental Illness in West African Students', *Social Psychiatry*, 1968, pp. 7–13.

46. Gordon, E. B., *op cit*, 1965.

47. Carpenter, L. and Brockington, 'A study of mental illness in Asians, West Indians, and Africans living in Manchester', *British Journal of Psychiatry*, Vol. 137, pp. 201–205.

48. Editorial, 'Paranoia and Immigrants', *British Medical Journal*, Vol. 281, 1980, pp. 1513–1514.

49. Cox, J. L., 'Aspects of Transcultural Psychiatry', *British Journal of Psychiatry*, Vol. 130, 1977, pp. 211–221.

50. Ballard, R., 'Ethnic Minorities and Social Sciences' in Khan, U. S. (ed.), *Minority Families in Britain*, Macmillan, London, 1979.

51. Hitch, P., *New Community*, ix, 2, 1981, pp. 256–262.

52. Alexander, B., *Nursing Times*, Vol. 17, 1974, pp. 632–636.

53. Interview with a psychiatrist in Liverpool, 19 October 1981.

54. *The Guardian*, 17 March 1981.

55. Ibid, 23 March 1981.

56. Leff, J. P., 'Transcultural Influences on Psychiatrists' Rating of Verbally Expressed Emotion', *British Journal of Psychiatry*, Vol. 125, 1974, pp. 336–340.

57. Rack, P. H., 'Immigrant Families and the Health Service', in Khan, U. S., *op cit*.

58. Szasz, T., *op cit*, 1974, p. 14.

59. Little, A., *Five Views of Multiracial Britain*, BBC, 1978, p. 57.

60. Burke, Aggrey W., 'Transcultural Psychiatry: Racism and Mental Illness', *The International Journal of Social Psychiatry*, Vol. 30/1 and 2, 1984, p. 50.

61. Hartman, P. and Husband, C., *Racism and the Mass Media*, Davis Poynter, 1974, p. 36.

62. Husband, C. (ed.), *Race in Britain: Continuity and Change*, Hutchinson, 1982, p. 20.

63. Rack, P. H., *Race Culture and Mental Disorder*, p. 124.

64. Burke, Aggrey W., 'The Consequence of Unplanned Repatriation', *British Journal of Psychiatry*, 123, 1973, (577): 109.

65. Mahy, G., 'The Psychotic West Indian Returns from England', International Congress of Transcultural Psychiatry, Bradford, 1976.

66. Rack, P. H., *op cit*, pp. 221–222.

67. Gordon, E. B., *op cit*, 1965.

68. Hemsi, L. K., *op cit*, 1967.

69. Mahy, G. *op cit*, 1976.

70. Black Health Workers and Patient Group, 'Psychiatry and the Corporate State', *Race and Class*, 1983.

71. Szasz, T. *op cit*, 1974, p. xiv.

72. Bandung File, *Mental Health*, Channel 4 TV, 7 November 1987.

73. Harris, G. *et al*, 'Mental Disorders in Afro-Caribbean Patients', *Psychological Medicine*, October 1988.

74. Ibid.

75. Bandung File, *op cit.*

76. Harris, G. *et al*, *op cit.*

77. Harmeed Ambreen, 'Black and Blue', *New Statesman and Society*, 21 April 1989.

78. Bandung File, *op cit.*

79. Ibid.

80. Bandung File, *op cit.*

81. Rooney, B., Research Paper on Mental Illness, Sociology Department Liverpool University, 1988.

82. Goldberg, D., *The Detection of Psychiatric Illness by Questionnaire*, OUP, 1972.

83. Staples, R., *Introduction to Black Sociology*, McGraw-Hill, 1976.

84. Beech, David, *Social Work and Mental Disorders*, Pepar, 1986, p. 70.

85. Ibid, p. 72.

86. Goffman, E., quoted in Morgan, M. *et al*, *Sociological Approaches to Health and Medicine*, Croom Helm, 1985.

87. Morgan, M. *et al*, *op cit.*

Part Three

# The Fruits of Action Research

# I. The Fruits of Action Research

In 1988 as a result of growing concern amongst local Black Community representatives, the City Council agreed to commission an inquiry into community and race relations in the Liverpool 8 area. This inquiry, led by Lord Gifford Q.C. together with Wally Brown and Ruth Bundy, was given a wide ranging brief to look into and report on issues affecting the Liverpool 8 area and to make recommendations for action to be taken by appropriate statutory, non-statutory and voluntary agencies in the city. It was felt that too often an inquiry or investigation was conducted *after* a serious disturbance had occurred and the inquiry by Lord Gifford, Q.C., was to avoid such a 'post mortem' situation in this instance.

The inquiry team spent several months meeting and discussing with a very wide range of people and representatives of local organisations, statutory and non-statutory agencies and as a result a first report on this work was produced and is published in book form entitled *Loosen the Shackles*.[1] This first report makes a large number of recommendations on the major issues affecting the Liverpool 8 area: employment and the economy, education, health, housing, social services, community services and policing.

The Report of the inquiry team was submitted to and given preliminary consideration by the Liverpool City Council and it was agreed that a Working Party of senior politicians should be established to draw up the Council's response to the issues raised in the Report which were of particular concern to the City Council. A major report which contained the views of Chief Officers of the Council was prepared for the Working Party. It is significant to note that the section on community services refers to several initiatives and proposals with which the action researchers on this Health and Race Project have had close involvement in various ways. For example, the Report mentions developments in relation to the Somali Community and states the fact that the Council has agreed to provide financial support to the Somali Women's Group (£9,212 in 1989/90) and is considering grant aid (capital £35,000–£40,000 and revenue £7,000 in 1989/90) to cover the refurbishment of a building to provide a centre or base for the Merseyside Somali Community Association. Consultative

F

Paper Three above describes the involvement of the action researchers and raises the issues now addressed by the Council.

The Council's response to the Gifford Inquiry Report also makes mention of the approval which had been given towards the conversion and refurbishment of premises in Upper Parliament Street for the Granby Community Mental Health Group to establish a Drop-In Centre for mentally disturbed black people. Approximately £180,000 capital was agreed and consideration was being given to funding the running costs of the centre. People in the black community have identified a number of important issues concerning the needs of black mentally ill people in Liverpool, and Consultative Paper Six above discusses these issues in Liverpool against the national experience black people have of psychiatric services.

A third initiative mentioned was the establishment within the City Council of a Translation and Interpreting Service. The service is funded mainly by the City Council but contributions are also made by the Liverpool Health Authority and Merseyside Improved Houses. The service provides an important resource for statutory agencies and others which have the responsibility to communicate either in writing or verbally with those for whom English is not their mother tongue. Again, as Consultative Paper Four shows, action research was involved in helping to identify and substantiate the need for this service, and representatives of the Health and Race Project jointly organised the Day Conference in July 1988 which gave the opportunity for representatives of the black community, statutory and non-statutory organisations to consider the details of the service required in Liverpool.

There has been a strong link between the work of action researchers and the development of the above services. At one level therefore the initiatives can be regarded as the 'fruits of action research'. However, there are three main reasons why it would be inappropriate for action researchers to claim total responsibility. Firstly, many other individuals and representatives of agencies have played their valuable part in enabling these proposals to reach fruition. In this respect the fruits of action research cannot be claimed by the researchers no matter how much they might have been involved in cultivating the ideas which have led to the establishment of the initiatives. This is not a discouragement to would-be action researchers. On the contrary, the absence of researcher ownership is a definite mark of a successful action research project.

Action research is not mainly about collecting statistics and compiling them for publications which are then claimed by the researcher for presentation at academic conferences. This is not to say that the collection of statistics and the production of publications or indeed participation in academic discourse is excluded or prohibited. But these are not the main objectives. The role of the researcher is to investigate issues affecting the community and using the results of that investigation, to work towards changing or influencing policies in order to redress the balance. This process cannot be set into motion unless researchers work with the community affected by the existing policies and practices, as well as with organisations with the responsibility to meet the needs of the community. It is this joint action which produces the fruits in action research.

Secondly, the actual process of providing the service needed is not within the power of researchers or pressure groups. They have no financial resources and even marginal funding such as Innercity Partnership grants is controlled by local statutory agencies. In the case of Innercity Partnership funding, voluntary organisations can only have grants for the maximum of four years. After this period the appropriate statutory agency – City Council or Health Authority – may take over the total financing of the initiative, and if they don't, the service may come to an end. This relationship with funding means that initiatives resulting from the work of researchers or other independent voluntary organisations tend to fall under the ambit of the funding body. They become, in common parlance, what the funding body provides. In a way, this could be regarded as 'legitimate ownership'. There are instances however, when the ownership is stretched to the extreme when some members of an organisation, desperate to present a progressive public image, lay unwarranted claims on initiatives of voluntary agencies even before they take over the full financing of the scheme. This remains the case even if such members had vehemently opposed the establishment of the scheme. This falls outside the scope of legitimacy as defined above and can aptly be described as 'Credit Stealing Syndrome' (CSS).

CSS is a familiar feature of many organisations. It affects individuals as well as groups and it takes different forms. One common form is when a statutory organisation picks up an idea from a voluntary organisation from an application form for grant aid or from arguments with representatives of outside organisations. The authority opposes or refuses to co-operate in the establishment of the initiative as described by the voluntary sector, and then later, proceeds to initiate the same scheme, albeit watered down, in the statutory sector. This does not happen only between statutory and voluntary organisations. It can be within a single organisation where there is a resistance to accepting suggestions for change emanating from radical, and therefore possibly marginalised, members in an essentially conservative or reactionary organisation. Such ideas often materialise later as proposals conceived by those in positions to make decisions within an organisation. The practice of this is illustrated below by a short case study of the development and work of Granby Mental Health Group to establish a Drop-In Centre.

Another form CSS takes is related to temporary employment contracts. The employing agency encourages employees in this category to develop ideas and schemes which are innovative and earn credit for the agency. Once these have been firmly incorporated into the functioning of the organisation, funding for the innovator mysteriously becomes a problem and the contract is not renewed. The removal of the initiator leaves the organisation free and safe to take total credit for the schemes developed or ideas pursued which are then handed to the new incumbent of the post. Many black people will be familiar with this situation. Some have maintained campaigns and called for collective action to fight against this form of injustice. What is difficult to fight, however, is the whole process of 'psychological lynching'[2] which can take place long before the termination of the post. The following are just some of the techniques employed in this process.

1. Exclusion from organisational meetings. This is achieved in a number of ways. Times of meetings are arranged when it is known that the targeted person is not able to attend; when inviting people to a meeting, the eyes of the invitor do not include the person. When arranging the next meeting everyone except the targeted person is asked whether or not the proposed date and time would be suitable. These non-verbal techniques do not only undermine confidence but also leave the person so affected psychologically isolated yet with no tangible cause for challenging the 'lynchers'. There are, of course, some people who speak out against this form of attack and challenge it every time it happens. But they end up being labelled the 'trouble makers' and they find themselves promoted to the next stage of the process i.e. the 'Banana Skin Syndrome'. At this level everyone is waiting to trip them up – one little mistake, and they have had it. The psychological pressure created by having to watch over your shoulder all the time becomes so intense that some people either develop a 'break-down' or they

decide to leave the organisation even before the post is terminated. Others, however, continue to fight with less energy spent looking over their shoulders, they know the blows are going to come and only look to identify who has delivered them, and in many instances find themselves echoing Caesar's words:'Et tu, Brute'.

2. In some instances a person finds that in meetings where people discuss their areas of work, someone else explains and elaborates on his/her work. It is as if people do not believe or accept that the individual is capable of articulating his/her own views or opinions. Of course nobody ever puts it as crudely as that. Usually it comes out in polite neatly packaged phrases such as 'I think what X means is . . .' to which the others respond, 'Oh yes, I see now what X means'. The discussion then carries on with the views and opinions of X on his/her work totally ignored, the emphasis laid on the interpretations of what others think X meant.

3. Another form of psychological lynching is trivialization of the targeted person's contributions in meetings. One way of achieving this is to make a joke of the suggestion and refuse to treat it seriously. Another way is to follow the suggestion with something totally different, as if the person has said nothing at all. Nobody in the group says, 'hang on a minute, let us just look at what X has just said'. This, if repeated, eventually makes the person feel that his/her contributions are not important.

4. A more damaging way in which psychological lynching operates is when everything the targeted person says or suggests is questioned and doubts are expressed about the credibility of the information offered. There is demand for evidence and in academic circles the usual 'go and write a paper on it and present your case at the next meeting' is an effective way of destroying the opposition. If the person is naive enough not to recognise this response for what it is, and does present a paper, the focus shifts from the points raised to the academic status of the paper and through this manoeuvre, the academic standard of a person is questioned. On the other hand, if one refuses to produce a paper the organisation is vindicated because the ball is in one's court. If no progress is made it is because the individual has failed to move it forward by producing the required paper. Either way the targeted person loses and is undermined.

5. In some instances, the targeted person may find that those in positions of power and decision making have given his/her work to other people with no prior consultation or discussion. People who

find themselves in this position gradually discover that they have been left without an effective job and thus the organisation minimises its guilt when the post is terminated.

6. Eye contact avoidance is another way of excluding people in a discussion. This happens even when the person has asked the question. The respondent to the question avoids addressing the targeted person through eye contact.

Although we have presented the above techniques in relation to a specific group of people i.e. those in temporary employment, the same techniques are used against a whole range of people who are deemed unacceptable in their respective organisations for a variety of reasons. In other words, if one becomes a target of elimination these tactics will be employed in varying degrees.

But among the veterans in CSS are thousands of researchers in academic institutions who watch helplessly as their hard earned data is published under the name of their supervisors. In many instances they are not even allowed to use the material to further their own academic qualifications if they have been employed as researchers. Even students researching for their higher degrees have discovered that the supervisor is using their material in national and international conferences without acknowledging it as the student's work. There are, of course, exceptions but the journey up the academic ladder for some is often paved with the sweat and tears of researchers.

There is however, a more disturbing and perhaps fundamental reason for the prevalence of CSS in organisations. What is being revealed is the practice which Schon calls 'Dynamic Conservatism'.[3] In this phenomenon, organisations only incorporate or accede to change to a minimum degree, sufficient to meet their own self interest and, as we have discussed earlier, to repel pressures for change which are being felt from outside. This usually means that when the idea which has been stolen from the voluntary sector or from the opposition is enacted by the statutory body, it lacks the vital characteristics which would have produced the required change. To ensure that this remains a public image building exercise the organisation seeks out employees/members it can manipulate, people who are not likely to upset the status quo, and people prepared to operate within the conservative framework of the organisation.

The third reason why it would be inappropriate for researchers to lay a total claim on the fruits of action research is that the provision of services is not the responsibility of researchers. This is the role of local statutory organisations who have the resources, albeit constrained by Central Government, and who should have an overall picture to enable them to develop a coherent strategy, drawing from the work of available research material in various fields and in consultation with the communities affected by the inequalities. As part of a good code of practice, statutory organisations should set up their own evaluation projects to enable them to meet the needs of their consumers more effectively. Consultation and other forms of liaison should extend to non-statutory and voluntary groups to ensure a city-based action plan to meet the needs of their communities. There are encouraging passages in the City Council's Report in response to the Gifford Inquiry which suggests that the City Council is beginning to move in this direction:

> 'This Report identifies a range of action which begins to develop a coherent strategy and action plan to address the needs of the black community in the city. It is essential to see all these measures as part of an integrated attack on racism and racial disadvantage in Liverpool. Whilst this Report has obviously concentrated upon the responsibilities and actions which the City Council itself can and should take, there are many agencies and organisations with which the Council will be able to work in pursuance of these objectives. Although the elimination of racism and the achievement of racial justice and equality will not be an easy task, there is much to recommend the Council seeking to work in conjunction with other agencies and the Local Community towards these goals.'[4]

These are encouraging words which it is hoped will be matched by the action taken.

This discussion has so far argued that researchers cannot take total credit for the fruits of action research. They have neither the financial resources nor the statutory obligation to set up needed services. The major reward or fruit of their activity lies in witnessing the successful development of an initiative in which they have been actively involved. That process of involvement begins with the identification of the shortfalls in service delivery, the compilation of information from that investigation; the presentation of that information to the relevant organisation; the making of recommendations for action and joining in the struggle to develop the needed service. These stages are not put forward as a blue print of how to conduct action research. They are, however, describing the route followed in the Health and Race Project. That route has not been an easy one, and the degree of difficulty depended on the extent to which the researchers gained the co-operation, not only of the Black Community but of the organisations under pressure to provide the needed services. In the development of the Translation and Interpreting Service and the Granby Community Mental Health Drop-In Centre the level of co-operation has varied considerably, as the following pages will show.

## References

1. Gifford, A. *et al*, *Loosen the Shackles: First Report of the Liverpool 8 Inquiry into Race Relations in Liverpool*, Karia Press, 1989.
2. This phrase was used by someone in a conference. Unfortunately, I cannot remember the name of that person. I offer my apologies.
3. Schon, Donald A., *Beyond the Stable State*, Temple Smith, 1971, p. 32.
4. Mellor, Nigel and Chape, Alan, *City Council Response to the First Report of the Liverpool 8 Inquiry in Race Relations in Liverpool*, Liverpool City Council, 1990.

# II. The Translation and Interpreting Service

As with several of the working papers, the results of the evaluation of the Health Authority's interpreting service were circulated to relevant agencies. These included the City Council, Liverpool Health Authority, Family Practitioner Committee and the Local Medical Committee. These are major public organisations with an obligation to provide services and to ensure that they have an effective communication system for all those who consume their services. The results of the survey have revealed that there is a very serious problem of communication between the providers of health services and those whose mother tongue is not English. Of the organisations circulated with the working paper, the City Council responded promptly and favourably even though the case studies cited in the paper related to the health service. The Council's response was in part due to its own awareness of communication problems, particularly with the newly arrived Vietnamese Community, and in part to a climate favourable to race issues within the Council following the Militant's regime.

The task of persuading the City Council of the need for a city-based Translation and Interpreting Service was taken up by the Community Liaison Officer who drafted a proposal outlining such a service. The proposal was distributed to relevant black organisations, statutory and non-statutory agencies for their comments. In general the comments were favourable and supportive of the proposal and it was consequently agreed that a conference should be held jointly by the Health and Race Project, the City Council and the Merseyside Community Relations Council. This Conference was held on 4th July 1988 and was attended by many representatives of black organisations; statutory and non-statutory agencies.

At the end of the conference it was agreed that a working party should be established and its task was to discuss in detail the form the service was to take in Liverpool. The City Council remained constructive in its posture, accepting the proposal but suggesting that an approach be made to other organisations both public and private for a contributution towards the cost of providing the service. In addition, it was suggested that the City should approach the Home Office for grant aid under Section II.

Of the organisations approached for financial support the Health Authority agreed to contribute £5,000 revenue and £2,000 capital in the 1989/90 period. Merseyside Improved Housing agreed to a £1,000 contribution. A discouraging response came from the Family Practitioner Committee which declined to make any contribution and later suggested it would set up its own interpreting service. This position was taken despite the Committee's stated commitments to the guidelines in the NAHA Report and its stated intention to look at the needs of 'ethnic minorities' in Liverpool. Following a number of letters from the Ethnic Minorities Health Group, the City Council, the Health and Race Project and others deploring the attitude of the Committee towards the project, it eventually agreed to contribute £500 towards the service and along with other organisations indicated its willingness to use the service once it has been established.

The hoped for financial support from the Home Office did not materialise as the Home Secretary had instigated a major review of Section II funding. It therefore became the responsibility of the City Council to find the majority of the initial sum of £60,500 needed to establish the service. The contributions from representatives at the conference and the Committee Reports written by the Community Liaison Officer for the Council, which show how the work developed following the conference are published in a report entitled *A Translation and Interpreting Service for Merseyside*.[1]

The Translation and Interpreting Service was set up in January 1990. The staff consists of a Co-ordinator and an Assistant Co-ordinator with the post of clerical assistant to be filled. The first report of the Co-ordinator states that there were 27 interpreters and translators on the register and between them they covered the ten commonly used languages on Merseyside: Chinese; Arabic; Punjabi; Swahili; Hindi; Somali; Urdu; Bengali, Vietnamese and Gujurati. In addition the service is also able to cater for European languages where required. The service had not been officially advertised and yet, as the list of requests shows, there is unequivocal evidence that this is a greatly needed provision. In the course of this project it will now be possible to give statistical figures and draw meaningful conclusions based not only on researcher's assessments and assumptions, but also on the numbers of clients using the service. This is action research in practice and it is hoped that the same approach will be adopted in the Drop-In Centre project to which we now turn.

# References

1. Mellor, Nigel *et al*, *A Translation and Interpreting Service for Merseyside*, Community Liaison Section, Liverpool City Council, 1990.

# III. The Granby Community Mental Health Drop-In Centre

The idea of a Drop-In Centre for mentally disturbed black people was first introduced by the Black Women's Group, now known as the Black Sisters, in the early 1980's. Members of the group were concerned about the problems facing mentally ill black people, some of whom were outpatients, whose needs were not being addressed by statutory bodies nor by existing voluntary organisations. Such patients were not involved in, nor were they utilising the facilities of Day Care Centres, most of which were situated in white areas. Some members of the Black Women's Group became involved in voluntary counselling in an attempt to ease the tensions and frustrations experienced by the patients. Some of those counselled were young women who were themselves members of the group. Racism was identified as a contributory factor in the origin of the stresses experienced. The racist treatment received in hospitals and the subsequent reluctance to be involved in existing Day Care Centres were also identified by both the counsellors and the counselled. Members of the group felt strongly that there was an urgent need for a Drop-In Centre in the Liverpool 8 area where black people could feel free to discuss their personal anxieties, problems and crises in an unstructured and non-judgmental atmosphere, a space where they could safely express their frustration and anger about the racism they experience in all aspects of their lives. In 1984 the Group approached a number of organisations for help towards the development of the Centre: Liverpool Housing Trust to identify suitable accommodation; Mencap, MIND, and the Social Services Department for advice and guidance on mental health issues; the Housing Corporation, Merseyside County Council and Mental Health Foundation for financial assistance. Despite all the hard work by the Group no progress was made.

In 1986 Merseyside Community Relations Council (MCRC) became very concerned about the continuing problems faced by black people in the field of mental health and more particularly about the experience of one young black mentally handicapped man in an institution for the mentally handicapped. This led to renewed efforts to secure funding not only for the Drop-In Centre but also for a residential hostel. A decision was made to apply for funding to the Innercity Partnership through the Liverpool Health Authority. It was agreed that at this stage only the Drop-In Centre should be established. Since the Group, now made up of MCRC and Black Sisters, had at that time no constitution and therefore no charitable status the application had to be submitted under the auspices of MIND and MCRC. It was at this point that researchers from the Health and Race Project joined the group.

In order to ensure that the application form was filled in properly, the group invited to its meeting personnel from the Liverpool Health Authority Planning administration section to help provide guidelines and points of clarification on how to complete the application form. The application was submitted for funding in 1987/88.

Along with other submissions, this application was considered by the Health Authority at its meeting on 25th November 1986 but it was not given priority for funding for two reasons. Firstly, the Health Authority wanted more detailed information on the capital costs. Secondly, the Group was informed that the Central and Southern Division of Psychiatry, had 'expressed some concern at aspects of the scheme' and had asked to be able to comment in detail on the proposals. On the first point a representative of another voluntary sector health organisation who was involved in the sponsoring group, expressed surprise and concern since some of his previous applications with less information had had no similar demands from the Health Authority. On the second question concerning the Division of Psychiatry comments, the same representative wrote to the Health Authority stating that since the project had had no sight of their objections, the Group had no opportunity to make clarification.

The required detailed information was promptly sent to the Health Authority and in a letter on the 22nd January 1987 the Health Authority expressed satisfaction with the information and confirmed that these costs had been sent to Merseyside Task Force on 15th January 1987 'with the comment that the C & S Division of Psychiatry had no further comments on the scheme'.

Since, according to this letter, 'all outstanding items have, therefore, now been resolved', and the Authority believed this would enable the Task Force 'to give consideration to this scheme together with the other submissions', the Group assumed that the application was now on the priority list. However, since doubts had been raised by the Health Authority's response to the initial application this motivated the group to approach the Task Force directly in order to explain why there was such an urgent need for the centre.

At a meeting with the Task Force, held on 31st March 1987, the Group was told that the Health Authority had not put the scheme on the priority list. Had this been done it would have been considered for the 1987/88 funding. However, not even all those projects on the priority list could be funded because of a drastic reduction in the budget. But this did not affect those projects which, like the Health and Race Project, were already in operation and only needed an extension. At this meeting the researchers, who were part of the Group, were reassured that there would be no problems in securing a further two years' funding for the Health and Race Project provided the Health Authority put it forward for funding. At the meeting in March, the Task Force representative reported on an earlier discussion with the Health Authority on 10th February 1987 when the Health Authority had been asked to draw up a new list with fewer but urgent projects for funding. At the Group's meeting with the Task Force in March 1987 this list had still not been presented by the Health Authority. A Task Force Senior Officer assured the Group that if the Drop-In Centre and the Health and Race Project were on this new list, they would be funded as he too now understood the need for these services. The list had to be submitted no later than April 1987.

When the list of approved schemes was announced later that year neither the Drop-In Centre, nor the Health and Race Project were on the list. Nor were two other projects which were addressing the needs of black people in the field of health – the Neighbourhood Health Project based in the Liverpool 8 area and the Health Authority's own submission for a post of a Race Relations Officer in Health. On the 9th of September, 1987 representatives from the first three projects held another meeting with the Task Force to find out why all these projects had failed to secure funding. The Task Force Senior Officer maintained his original statement: 'We don't take all decisions ourselves. The Health Authority gives us guidelines.' The rejection of all the projects addressing race issues moved the whole debate to a political level and the Group turned to the City Council for assistance. The Chair of the Race Sub-Committee convened a meeting in 1987 with the Task Force, the Health Authority and representatives from the Granby Community Mental Health Group, the Health and Race Project, the Neighbourhood Health Project and the Racial Minorities Health Group. At the end of two hours of accusations and counter accusations the Task Force agreed to give a small sum of money – £4,000 – to allow one part-time worker to continue the work of the Health and Race Project for the 1987/88 period and promised full funding for two full-time workers for 1988/90. The Health Authority indicated that they would be more than willing to consider another application for a Drop-In Centre. But since the Centre would be a Community Health Service its funding could also be secured from Task Force through the City Council. The Group opted for this avenue and approached the Social Services Department which put forward a proposal to the City Council for financial support towards the establishment of a Drop-In Centre. However, this proposal together with two other projects in favour of specific organisations were outside the allocation of financial support for community, voluntary black and other non statutory organisations. The Council therefore did not approve the project at this stage but increased the overall allocation from half to three quarters of a million pounds. This alteration was intended to enable the Granby Community Mental Health Group proposal to be considered in the light of other competing demands for financial support within the 1988/89 Urban Programme Voluntary Sector Allocation.

At this stage the City Council became embroiled in a long argument with Central Government because of the stance taken by the former with regards to the Employment Training Scheme. This caused a long delay in dealing with funding from the Urban Programme in 1988. In the summer of that year the Granby Community Mental Health Group was able to identify a suitable building owned by the Council for the centre, and the Community Liaison Officer reported to the Urban Programme Sub-Committee on 4th November 1988 on the request to purchase the property and it was agreed that:

> 'the City Estates Surveyor be requested to negotiate and report upon the most suitable terms for the use of 91 Upper Parliament Street by the group and that a full report including detailed costings for the project be submitted to this committee as soon as possible.'
> (Urban Programme Sub-Committee – Minute 61)

The Group was then in a position to commission Liverpool Housing Trust to conduct a feasibility study on the building and the results together with summary information on staffing and running costs were forwarded to the Council's Community Liaison Officer who presented a further report to the Urban Programme Sub-Committee at its meeting on 9th February 1989. Further discussions were held between the City Council and Task Force and this enabled the Council at its meeting on 8th March 1989 to approve grant aid to the Granby Community Mental Health Group and instruct the City Estates Surveyor to dispose of the property at 91 Upper Parliament Street to the Group; grant aid was to be increased in order to include the purchase of a long lease.

However, when the detailed proposal was submitted to the Task Force by the City Council, approval for the scheme was not given for two reasons. Firstly, it was suggested that further consultation was needed with the Health Authority. Secondly it was argued that it was not possible to start sufficient work on the building to charge a significant amount of expenditure to the 1988/89 Urban Programme funding. The Task Force then suggested that the Council should re-submit the project for the 1989/90 funding. This was a depressing development for the group as it was widely known that there was little scope for new projects in the whole of the Council's programme for the 1989/90 period. There was only £2.3 million available for new projects and the schemes put forward needed a budget of £40 million. This situation was made worse by the strict rules placed by Central Government on a Local Authority's use of Urban Programme money. The Government insisted that support should go towards capital projects rather than revenue and that at least 40% of the funds should be directed to economic projects rather than social welfare schemes. When, therefore, the Council at its meeting on 1st June 1989 stated that:

'Urgent discussions be held with the Merseyside Task Force and the Health Authority with the view to ensuring that urban pro-gramme resources are made available in 1989/90 for the estab-lishment of the Granby Community Mental Health Group Drop-In Centre,'

the Group suspected that this was yet another attempt to frustrate its application for financial support. It therefore asked to be represented at this meeting with the Task Force and the Health Authority, just in case either needed reminding about the history of the project. At the meeting it was not clear why this consultation was needed since neither the Task Force nor the Health Authority had forgotten the heated discussions of the previous year when the Health Authority declined to put the Drop-In Centre on the priority list. It could be that the Health Authority had since taken a very keen interest in the mental health needs of black people in Liverpool and was itself thinking of submitting a scheme for Innercity Partnership funding. This will be dealt with later. At the meeting the Health Authority raised no objection and the Task Force asked the City Council to submit the Drop-In Centre scheme for funding. The results of the discussion were presented to the Council's Urban Programme Sub-Committee at its meeting on 15th August 1989 and the proposal to fund the project for capital costs on a phased basis was approved. A submission to this effect was forwarded to the Task Force and the scheme was eventually approved on 17th October 1989. The total grant for capital costs was £181,000. £25,000 of this amount was for the purchase of the 99 year lease for the building and the rest was for the refurbishment of the property and equipment. In the 1990/91 submission, the Council included revenue costs for the centre – £100,000 a year for four years. This too has now been approved.

As with the negotiations with the City Council over the development of the Translation and Interpreting Service, the Community Liaison Officer played an important role in various ways. He prepared several reports to Committee at different stages of the project and the Group also received support and much more helpful information and advice on other matters which were to prove of great assistance throughout.

When events are reported chronologically, as above, they can appear simple, straightforward and uncomplicated. They lose the fraught climate within which they occurred. But as anyone who has been involved in trying to persuade an organisation to support a scheme whose objective is to meet the needs of black people knows, this is not an easy or simple task. It is in the process of this persuasion that different forms of resistance are encountered. The City Council is made up of members belonging to different political parties as well as officers who manage the Departments. Although at an organisational level there may have been public acceptance that there was a need for a Drop-In Centre for mentally ill black people, there were nevertheless individuals who did not support the scheme wholeheartedly. Nobody openly declared opposition to the establishment of the Centre. But then people do not have to since there are more effective ways of achieving the same objectives without being labelled racist. Questions were raised and doubts expressed. 'If all that amount of money is spent on one project what will happen to the rest of the projects in the City?' A valid question. But if the organisation believed, as it appeared to, that there was an urgent need to provide such a facility for black people in the City, then resources should be made available for what the organisation regarded as a priority. Within the Labour Group there were still elements of the militant tendency and there were still queries, albeit subdued, about the

Centre being preferential treatment for black people. Other people attacked the Group by insinuating that it was approaching various sources for financial support – simply trying to grab as much money as it could. Others questioned the need for the Granby Community Mental Health Drop-In Centre since a similar Drop-In Centre was being established nearby by the City Social Services Department. The fact that all other existing Day Care Centres for mentally ill people which were being provided by the statutory service were ineffective in meeting the needs of black people seemed to have escaped their notice.

All these questions and doubts by people in positions of power, and able to squash the grant, created a lot of pressure for the Group. A great deal of time and energy was spent by members of the Group in trying to find and lobby Councillors who were sympathetic to the project. This took the form of phone calls late at night and early in the morning in an attempt to catch Councillors at home; visits to the City Council to try to catch them at work and repeated visits to their surgeries.

To gain more support the Group enlisted the help of the Mental Health Commissioners as well as the Director of Social Services. The former were not at first aware of the problem in terms of provision for black people in this area, but when representatives of the Group met them in one of their annual visits to Liverpool and drew their attention to the problem, they decided to come to the Group's meeting and after that visit, gave their full support to the project. The Director of Social Services also gave his support to the project and acknowledged the need for such a provision in order to improve the effectiveness of Day Care Centres in meeting the needs of black people in the city.

As always, the external pressure in turn created tension and conflict within the Group and as a result some members left, leaving others to weather the tension and shoulder all the work involved in securing support for the Centre.

It is not known when the Health Authority developed an interest in the mental health needs of black people in Liverpool. It was certainly not before the beginning of 1987, as at that time their senior representative told the Joint Care Planning Team sub-group for people with mental illness that he was not aware of any problems in caring for ethnic minorities with a mental illness. However, the Group became aware of the Health Authority's interest in May 1989 when the Authority invited a number of people from different organisations to a meeting to discuss the mental health needs of black people in

Liverpool with a view to securing funding from Innercity Partnership. The Granby Community Mental Health Group was not invited, but a researcher with the Health and Race Project, who was not associated with the Group, was invited. The researcher declined the invitation to attend the Meeting and suggested that it was more appropriate for the Granby Community Mental Health Group to attend, since the Group had been involved in this field for a long time. Eventually, following further expressions of concern regarding the Health Authority's intention in calling the meeting, representatives from the Granby Community Mental Health Group were invited to attend.

However, since it was not clear what issues were to be addressed, the Granby Community Mental Health Group asked to meet the appropriate representatives of the Health Authority to clarify matters first.

At this meeting, held on June 7 1989, what was uppermost in the members' minds was why the Granby Community Mental Health Group had been excluded from the initial invitation list. In an attempt to put the Group's mind at rest the representative of the Health Authority stated categorically that whilst he knew about the Drop-In Centre proposal he did not know about the existence of the Granby Community Mental Health Group, because when the 1987/88 submission for the Drop-In Centre had been made, it had not been in the name of that group. This was a real puzzle to the Group. It had not been expected that every Officer of the Health Authority would know about the Group, but certain factors made their omission from the invitation list seem inexplicable.

Firstly, it was considered reasonable to expect that since the Health Authority had established a Race Relations Advisory Committee in order to conduct this work effectively, it would have an up-to-date list of organisations which were active in or concerned about the health needs of the black community.

Secondly, it was known that the Granby Community Mental Health Group had been referred to in meetings of the Health and Race Project at which the Health Authority had been well represented.

Thirdly, it was also clear that the minutes of the Health and Race Project had been sent to the Race Relations Advisory Committee of the Health Authority.

Fourthly, there was also evidence to suggest that the activities of the Granby Community Mental Health Group had actually been discussed at the Race Relations Advisory Committee.

Even though all these various points were put to the Health Authority representative, he was adamant that he had no awareness of the Group's existence and so the meeting ended on a negative and frustrating note.

This account, along with other evidence presented in this Report, serves to illustrate a number of features about the way in which large statutory organisations frequently relate with or regard voluntary organisations generally and black groups in particular.

Unfortunately, many large institutions see their relations with non statutory groups in a conflictual mode rather than seeking to develop a co-operative relationship with them. This may be partly due to the form of accountability adopted. Within large institutions, middle and senior management are recruited for their competence in their respective field of work. To admit to their supervisors, Board, or elected members that some groups of voluntary representatives have any valid awareness of the problem, still less any idea as to the kind of solutions which could be considered, would be seen as failure or an acknowledgment of inadequacy by the bureaucrat. Thus, the system encourages those employed by it to regard themselves as expert, those outside as wholly amateur. This has particularly serious implications when one considers that it is the people living in the community who are experiencing the adequacy or otherwise of the provision for those with mental health problems, who know at first hand what needs exist and from that uniquely valid experience are able to make contributions to the development of service provision. A further feature within bureaucracies which compounds this situation is the fact that accountability is usually upwards within the hierarchy of the Department rather than to the customer, client or community. Thus in order to progress within a large institution, an employee will need to impress his/her superior or office manager. It is usually very difficult to achieve this by continually siding with the community representatives who are generally seen as troublesome people who continually interfere with or disrupt what would otherwise be the normal smooth running of the bureaucratic machine. Thus accountability outside an institution is insidiously discouraged.

However, some of these styles and organisational characteristics are beginning to be challenged. The increasing pressure on large institutions to adopt equal opportunity policies and fair recruitment and selection techniques in employing staff has begun to increase black representation within large institutions. The mere presence of black staff, particularly in middle and senior management positions, can discourage some of the worst excesses of racism which have riddled many of these bodies for decades. More positively, such black staff can make their own particular contributions to the development of appropriate policies and sensitive services which more closely meet the needs of different groups in the community than hitherto. Their presence at any level within what were previously largely white institutions can be an encouragement to others to consider making application for employment and can serve as a positive role model.

There are signs that both the Health Authority and the City Council have begun to take some initial steps which could promote changes along these lines. It is important that such measures are not simply window-dressing, but are part of a comprehensive and integrated programme of action which impinges on all areas of the institutions' activities and at all levels of its decision-making and service provision. Otherwise the initiatives, however well intentioned, will at best be marginal and peripheral, at worst they will be seen as cynical attempts to 'buy off' the opposition or to defuse a difficult or tense situation. The key factor in all this is **accountability**. Unless and until large institutions see those for whom they provide services, and who in many cases also pay for the costs of the services they provide, as genuine consumers with rights and power, to whom they should be accountable, then the bureaucrat will continue to rule.

Despite all the problems facing the Group, funding was eventually secured. The refurbishment of the building was not without its difficulties but the issues surrounding them fall outside the immediate scope of this report and could be dealt with on another occasion.

# IV. Conclusions and Recommendations

It is common practice to draw conclusions and to offer recommendations at the end of a report. This, however, is not necessary in this instance since each of the Working Papers includes a description of the action necessary to address the problems which have been discussed. What is attempted here is to highlight some issues in relation to the experience of black people not only in the field of health but on a more general level, and to suggest how institutions, the community and individuals can begin to work together in an attempt to redress the imbalance and in doing so to start the process of devising strategies for radical change.

One of the points to be emphasized is the need to analyse the experience of black people not in a vacuum but in the social, political and economic context of class and gender, for it is only in this context that issues affecting black people can be identified, and strategies to deal with them can not only be formulated but can also be translated into action. In the process of identifying such issues, formulating strategies and translating them into practice, research has a crucial role to play. The research which fulfills this role most effectively is not the traditional, academic, value free research but committed action research whose results can be used as a tool for intervention at various levels in pursuit of justice and equality. Commitment here does not mean that researchers amend their findings in order to bring them into line with their own predilections or preconceptions. In common with other researchers those involved in action research should follow the same requirements of objectivity in the collection of their data and may indeed have to admit on occasions that their findings do not support the prevalent assumptions in the particular area in which they are involved. Commitment in research is about asking oneself a number of fundamental questions as for example: What determines the choice of area/subject to be researched? Whose interests will be served? To what use will the results be put? To what degree or to what level of intervention is the researcher prepared to commit her/himself? Just as important also are questions as to whether the research is likely to contribute to the empowerment of the groups researched or is likely to provide more ammunition with which to oppress them? These are not value-free questions. They confront every Social Science researcher. All researchers are value-laden and committed. The question is, committed to what? It is in the responses to the above questions that we can determine those who are committed to maintain the status quo and those who are prepared to challenge it.

Through the adoption of action research and in conjunction with many others who played their valuable parts two initiatives, the Translation and Interpreting Service and the Drop-In Centre, were established in the course of the project. The Drop-In Centre will provide a space where black people can feel free to express their anger about racism, can feel safe in discussing personal crises and problems, can behave in a way concomitant with their stressed feelings without being labelled schizophrenic or psychotic. By enabling people to express their frustration the Centre, it is hoped, will function as a preventative measure to mental illness. However, even if the Centre is successful in preventing the occurrence of 'breakdowns' it is important to remember that this does not in itself tackle or remove the injustices and the inequalities in society that creates the stress. Society remains racist, sexist and classist. Similarly the Translation and Interpreting Service will remove the barriers confronted by some black people whose mother tongue is not English. They will now have access to information on a wide range of resources available through Housing, Health Authority, Family Practitioner Committees etc. However, it is clear that simply having knowledge and understanding of what is available is far removed from sharing in what is available. What this knowledge does, however, is to make it crystal clear in one's own language that 'there is not a lot down for you pal'. This understanding could be the beginnings of some concerted action within the community to argue for a fairer share of resources available. When people understand the situation they might be in a position to do something about it. Knowledge is power. Withholding information and thereby limiting the knowledge people have of the real situation is the most effective way of oppression and organisations in general constantly employ this strategy.

Both these initiatives must therefore be seen in the context of an unequal society that discriminates and in which resources are not equally distributed. Such schemes have a useful role in terms of mitigating the effects of discrimination and raising awareness about the realities of inequalities, but they are no substitute for striking at the root cause of the symptoms they mitigate, and those are embedded in the wider social, political and economic structure, in the different institutions and organisations, both statutory and voluntary.

Too often the promotion of change, the achievement of equality and the marshalling of resources needed to achieve the change are dealt with in the context of debates and decisions which are peripheral to the main stream of local statutory organisations, e.g. Local Government and Health Authority. Thus, for example, Section II and Urban Programme are often used to fund initiatives which are seen as special or additional to mainstream activities. In this way they fail to challenge or change the traditional ways of doing things and as a result the organisation remains racist in its practice. It is therefore crucial that it is made very clear to these agencies that the promotion of equality and the eradication of discrimination must be a central part of the entire decision making process. This equally applies to Central Government as well as to the private and voluntary sectors. The achievement of equality would therefore require a number of things:

1. Quite often organisations under pressure to provide services defend themselves by pointing to lack of resources. It is therefore crucial that the first step to meaningful change is to accept the fact that the greatest contribution of resources would be those which are currently available within the organisation itself. It is imperative that these are used effectively, justly and fairly. In the words of W. W. Rostow, resources are not, they become.[1] If you really want to do something you will find the resources with which to do it.
2. It requires the acceptance and the preparedness to deal with the costs involved in implementing policies leading to equality. Those costs are both practical and ideological and they dominate at both personal and organisational levels.
3. It requires the building up of alliances. A range of committed people in various influential organisations which control resources must work together formally and informally on a wide range of issues in a way that can begin to promote the kind of change that is required. Alliances and not competition should be encouraged between the various oppressed groups. Those groups should then in turn work with local activists and other independent agencies with a broader perspective to form alliances with those committed people who control large influential institutions. These links must be formed to break the chains of oppression. In the area of employment, for example, it is evident that action is needed not only to ensure that racism and prejudice are eradicated from all employ-

ment and recruitment practices but real equality of opportunity must also be experienced by black pupils in the education system to tackle the persistent problem of underachievement. Progress in these areas will be attained most effectively through the establishment of a wide network to promote joint action by employers, black organisations, schools and others concerned about racial justice.

4. A way must be found to achieve an equal, fair distribution of resources by unlocking the stranglehold which various decision makers at various levels of organisations presently have. This will involve a thorough search for and closure of all the loopholes used to perpetuate discrimination despite various legislation to eradicate it.

5. Finally, it is crucial for committed people in influential positions to realise the importance of developing an expertise in taking with them in increasing numbers their colleagues and employees/members in a commitment to promoting change. The mechanisms for achieving this must be incorporated in the framework of the employment/membership conditions within which there would be a rewarding of positive results. Within that same framework it should be made quite clear that people who discriminate will be dealt with firmly. That knowledge will act as both a deterrent and a sanction. The success of this whole process will require a strong committed leadership from the top. The question to ask here is why should any leadership be committed to the eradication of discrimination and oppression, and the promotion of equality?

There are moral, political, economic and social reasons why inequalities should be eliminated in society. Discrimination destroys the moral fibre of society. It is a disease whose toxins poison both the oppressor and the oppressed. It runs counter to the constantly proclaimed principles of democracy, equality and justice and it is totally incompatible with truly humanistic or Christian values. One cannot seriously regard oneself as humanist or Christian and still practice or tolerate racism.

A society whose moral fibre is totally destroyed is sitting on a time bomb and is politically volatile. The oppressed will at some stage find means to express their frustration and find ways to liberate themselves. Those in positions of power know this, hence the need to keep the lid constantly on in the form of legislation, the police and the army. For that lid to be kept firmly on demands the deployment of resources and that in turn starves other sectors of society of those resources – an unhealthy political position to be in for any government. But the lid in any case cannot stay on for ever. In Britain the explosions have been intermittent in the form of riots. But the events in Eastern Europe and South Africa must serve as a lesson as to what the results of oppression could be.

The economic repercussions are well known to business. As Ramsey observed, the upset arising from oppression is not confined to the community. It spills over into the work place and makes industrial relations even more difficult.[2] But more importantly even a potential for disorder frightens business customers and this in turn leads to loss of jobs and profitability that industry needs. Discrimination also means that industry is not utilising talent from the whole community and therefore important jobs may be left short of labour. For all these reasons, it makes moral, political, social and economic sense for society and its institutions to work towards the elimination of discrimination. A society which is founded and feeds on exploitation and is not concerned about injustice and inequalities contains within itself the seeds of its own destruction.

## References

1. Rostow, W. W., *The Stages of Economic Growth*, Cambridge University Press, 1960.
2. Ramsey, Bob, 'Why Equal Opportunities? The Management Perspective', in Ben-Tovim, G. *et al*, *Equal Opportunities and the Employment of Black People and Ethnic Minorities on Merseyside*, Merseyside Area Profile Group, 1983.